# SAVING AND INVESTING

Financial Knowledge and Financial Literacy
that Everyone Needs and Deserves to Have!

## Michael Fischer

authorHOUSE®

*This book is a work of non-fiction. Unless otherwise noted, the author and the publisher make no explicit guarantees as to the accuracy of the information contained in this book and in some cases, names of people and places have been altered to protect their privacy.*

*The author does not want to take credit nor does he assume responsibility for anyone's investment successes or failures, although he clearly believes that financial education and financial literacy are the keys to achieving good saving and investing results and that this book will provide a huge step forward along the journey towards achieving this goal.*

*First published by AuthorHouse 9/26/07*

*ISBN: 1-4208-6696-6 (sc)*

*Library of Congress Control Number: 2005906185*

*Printed in the United States of America*
*Bloomington, Indiana*

*This book is printed on acid-free paper.*

*The first adition of this book was first published by AuthorHouse 9/28/2005*

*For Those who Dare to Dream*

# TABLE OF CONTENTS

# INTRODUCTION

**Money is incredibly important.** It allows us to live enjoyable, comfortable lives. We need money to pay for food, a bed, heating, a home, a car, perhaps tuition for our children's schools, vacations, and many other things that are so important. It is not greed that should drive us to learn about this subject – when almost everything we need and want costs money – we simply cannot ignore the importance of understanding money and of being able to manage our finances. **This is the case whether we like it or not - not focusing on this stuff does not make it go away – on the contrary, money usually becomes an issue when it is <u>not</u> thought about, and when there is <u>not</u> enough of it.**

**Unless we want to accumulate huge amounts of debt, earn every penny just before we spend it, or live very poorly in retirement, we need to save money and invest it! And how we save and how we invest has a major impact on how much we end up with.** Some people make large amounts of money but still end up with financial headaches as a result of not managing their finances properly, whilst other people that never made a lot of money own their own homes, enjoy great vacations, send their kids to great schools and lead lives free of financial worry. The difference is in the doing – how they save and invest!

**This subject is not just important – it is becoming more important all the time as we become increasingly responsible for managing our own finances.** Historically the government and employers played a larger role in looking after our saving and investing needs. Today, most governments are getting smaller and more efficient, not to mention that many are financially stretched themselves. Governments predominantly set up the framework for saving and investing through laws and tax rules - the actual decisions and actions are increasingly left to us. Saving and investing is also usually not the employer's core business and can create conflicts of interest – they are also increasingly outsourcing this. **The net result is that we better know what is going on.**

**Despite the importance of money, saving, investing and financial markets, most of us are never taught about these things.** Some of us try to build our knowledge through trial and error - often lots of errors. Many of us do not even try because we feel that the whole subject is just too overwhelming and too large to even start worrying about. When we do pick up snippets regarding this subject, they are often not well explained, or they are based on opinions that may or may not be true, as opposed to being the facts that should be the basis of any decision. Without the full picture, trying to understand what is going on is like trying to build a puzzle with a lot of missing and damaged pieces, and with no idea of how they connect.

**Fortunately, learning about saving, investing, and how our financial system works is straightforward.** One key is to get the complete picture. The other is to understand how things work, and not to focus on what is happening or what did happen, without understanding why this is or was the case. Many things exist in the financial world because they create win-win situations that provide benefits to all of the parties that take part in the transaction, and these things tend to happen over and over again. Understanding these and other fundamental concepts is crucial to understanding what is happening and what might happen next. These are the concepts that we are going to look at in this book. **They are also the concepts that have been used by anyone that has become rich and that has stayed that way.**

# Chapter I

# COMPOUNDING

**Compounding is probably the most important saving and investing concept that we are going to learn about.** Albert Einstein called it the $8^{th}$ wonder of the world and the most powerful force on earth! Compounding means repeatedly earning a return on an amount of money - as the amount of money grows with each return that is added, each subsequent return is larger than the last one and the money grows faster and faster. It is the snowball effect in action, and it is compounding that allows small amounts that we save to become large amounts.

Someone that has $1,000 and that can earn a 5% return per year will get 5% on $1,000 in Year 1, which is $50. He or she will start Year 2 with $1,050; the 5% return on this amount is $52.50. When this is added to the $1,050, he or she has the even larger sum of $1,102.50. In Year 3 he or she will earn 5% on $1,102.50, which is $55.13. Each year the amount saved grows, and it grows more quickly as shown in the following table.

| YEAR | BALANCE AT START OF YEAR | RATE OF RETURN | RETURN DURING YEAR | NEW TOTAL AT END OF YEAR |
|------|--------------------------|----------------|--------------------|--------------------------|
| 1    | 1,000.00                 | 5%             | 50.00              | 1,050.00                 |
| 2    | 1,050.00                 | 5%             | 52.50              | 1,102.50                 |
| 3    | 1,102.50                 | 5%             | 55.13              | 1,157.63                 |
| 4    | 1,157.63                 | 5%             | 57.88              | 1,215.51                 |
| 5    | 1,215.51                 | 5%             | 60.78              | 1,276.28                 |
| 6    | 1,276.28                 | 5%             | 63.81              | 1,340.10                 |
| 7    | 1,340.10                 | 5%             | 67.00              | 1,407.10                 |
| 8    | 1,407.10                 | 5%             | 70.36              | 1,477.46                 |
| 9    | 1,477.46                 | 5%             | 73.87              | 1,551.33                 |
| 10   | 1,551.33                 | 5%             | 77.57              | **$1,628.89**            |

We can see that in Year 10 the savings grew by $77.57, whereas in the first year they grew by $50 - the return in the tenth year is earned on the much larger sum of $1,551.33, a sum that includes the returns that were added to the $1,000 in all of the previous years. In this example of compounding, over ten years, $1,000 became $1,628.89.

After 20 years, the $1,000 would grow to:

| YEAR | BALANCE AT START OF YEAR | RATE OF RETURN | RETURN DURING YEAR | NEW TOTAL AT END OF YEAR |
|------|--------------------------|----------------|--------------------|--------------------------|
| 11   | 1,628.89                 | 5%             | 81.44              | 1,710.33                 |
| 12   | 1,710.33                 | 5%             | 85.52              | 1,795.85                 |
| 13   | 1,795.85                 | 5%             | 89.79              | 1,885.64                 |
| 14   | 1,885.64                 | 5%             | 94.28              | 1,979.93                 |
| 15   | 1,979.93                 | 5%             | 99.00              | 2,078.92                 |
| 16   | 2,078.92                 | 5%             | 103.95             | 2,182.87                 |
| 17   | 2,182.87                 | 5%             | 109.14             | 2,292.01                 |
| 18   | 2,292.01                 | 5%             | 114.60             | 2,406.61                 |
| 19   | 2,406.61                 | 5%             | 120.33             | 2,526.94                 |
| 20   | 2,526.94                 | 5%             | 126.35             | **$2,653.29**            |

If it were left to continue it would grow even more. The longer it compounds for, the more it grows, and the faster it grows. We can show how the money grows more quickly each year on a graph.

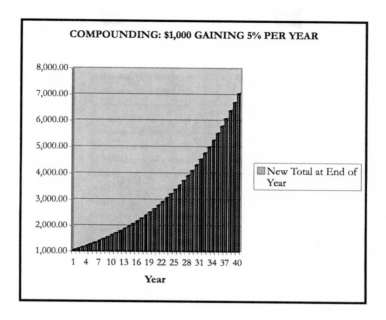

Starting early is important because it is time, and the returns that have already been added, that allow the money to grow more quickly. We can illustrate the difference starting earlier makes by looking at two imaginary people - *Abby* and *Zak*, who invest in the following ways:

- *Abby:* starts at age 25 and contributes $2,000 at the end of each year for 10 years - her total contribution is $20,000. At the end of 10 years, *Abby*, now 34, stops contributing and then does nothing except let her money continue compound at 5% until she is 55;
- *Zak:* starts at age 35 and contributes $2,000 at the end of each year for the next 20 years until he is 54. His total contribution is $40,000 and his contributions also compound at 5% per year.

The next table illustrates what *Abby* and *Zak* have at the end of each year and what they will have accumulated by age 55.

| AGE | ABBY | ZAK |
|---|---|---|
| 25 | **2,000.00** | |
| 26 | **4,100.00** | |
| 27 | **6,305.00** | |
| 28 | **8,620.25** | |
| 29 | **11,051.26** | |
| 30 | **13,603.83** | |
| 31 | **16,284.02** | |
| 32 | **19,098.22** | |
| 33 | **22,053.13** | |
| 34 | **25,155.79** | |
| 35 | 26,413.57 | **2,000.00** |
| 36 | 27,734.25 | **4,100.00** |
| 37 | 29,120.97 | **6,305.00** |
| 38 | 30,577.01 | **8,620.25** |
| 39 | 32,105.86 | **11,051.26** |
| 40 | 33,711.16 | **13,603.83** |
| 41 | 35,396.72 | **16,284.02** |
| 42 | 37,166.55 | **19,098.22** |
| 43 | 39,024.88 | **22,053.13** |
| 44 | 40,976.12 | **25,155.79** |
| 45 | 43,024.93 | **28,413.57** |
| 46 | 45,176.18 | **31,834.25** |
| 47 | 47,434.98 | **35,425.97** |
| 48 | 49,806.73 | **39,197.26** |
| 49 | 52,297.07 | **43,157.13** |
| 50 | 54,911.92 | **47,314.98** |
| 51 | 57,657.52 | **51,680.73** |
| 52 | 60,540.40 | **56,264.77** |
| 53 | 63,567.42 | **61,078.01** |
| 54 | 66,745.79 | **66,131.91** |
| 55 | **$70,083.08** | **$69,438.50** |

The numbers in bold show that contributions are being made – when the text is not bold, it means that the money is just compounding with no contributions.

**Amazingly, *Abby*, who only contributed for ten years, ended up with more money at 54 and at age 55 than *Zak*, who paid in for twenty years.** Starting early more than compensated for the fact that *Abby* only contributed for half the time period. (If she had continued to contribute, until she was 54 like Zak did, she would have ended up with $139,521.58 by age 55).

**Because starting early means that the money is compounded more often, starting early has a huge impact on the ultimate amount saved!**

What if we aren't 25 anymore and cannot start that 'early'? We can still be early by starting today, which is better than starting tomorrow. The principle applies whether we start at 25, 35, 45 or even at 55. Most of us will live much longer than we think. When we are young, we often think that we will never get old. The reality is that most of us will live for a very long time, and having had money compound in the background for all those years will make a huge difference.

Starting early and letting money compound for as long as possible is clearly very important. **The other key factor that impacts how much our money compounds to is the amount earned on the money each year – the return.** The higher the return, the greater the growth each year, and the larger the amount it compounds to. Let's look at the difference between earning 1% interest on $10,000 for 20 years and earning 3% interest on $10,000 for 20 years.

| | COMPOUNDING WITH 1% RETURN | | | COMPOUNDING WITH 3% RETURN | | |
|---|---|---|---|---|---|---|
| YEAR | BALANCE AT START OF YEAR | INTEREST DURING YEAR | NEW TOTAL AT END OF YEAR | BALANCE AT START OF YEAR | INTEREST DURING YEAR | NEW TOTAL AT END OF YEAR |
| 1 | 10,000.00 | 100.00 | 10,100.00 | 10,000.00 | 300.00 | 10,300.00 |
| 2 | 10,100.00 | 101.00 | 10,201.00 | 10,300.00 | 309.00 | 10,609.00 |
| 3 | 10,201.00 | 102.01 | 10,303.01 | 10,609.00 | 318.27 | 10,927.27 |
| 4 | 10,303.01 | 103.03 | 10,406.04 | 10,927.27 | 327.82 | 11,255.09 |
| 5 | 10,406.04 | 104.06 | 10,510.10 | 11,255.09 | 337.65 | 11,592.74 |
| 6 | 10,510.10 | 105.10 | 10,615.20 | 11,592.74 | 347.78 | 11,940.52 |
| 7 | 10,615.20 | 106.15 | 10,721.35 | 11,940.52 | 358.22 | 12,298.74 |
| 8 | 10,721.35 | 107.21 | 10,828.57 | 12,298.74 | 368.96 | 12,667.70 |
| 9 | 10,828.57 | 108.29 | 10,936.85 | 12,667.70 | 380.03 | 13,047.73 |
| 10 | 10,936.85 | 109.37 | 11,046.22 | 13,047.73 | 391.43 | 13,439.16 |
| 11 | 11,046.22 | 110.46 | 11,156.68 | 13,439.16 | 403.17 | 13,842.34 |
| 12 | 11,156.68 | 111.57 | 11,268.25 | 13,842.34 | 415.27 | 14,257.61 |
| 13 | 11,268.25 | 112.68 | 11,380.93 | 14,257.61 | 427.73 | 14,685.34 |
| 14 | 11,380.93 | 113.81 | 11,494.74 | 14,685.34 | 440.56 | 15,125.90 |
| 15 | 11,494.74 | 114.95 | 11,609.69 | 15,125.90 | 453.78 | 15,579.67 |
| 16 | 11,609.69 | 116.10 | 11,725.79 | 15,579.67 | 467.39 | 16,047.06 |
| 17 | 11,725.79 | 117.26 | 11,843.04 | 16,047.06 | 481.41 | 16,528.48 |
| 18 | 11,843.04 | 118.43 | 11,961.47 | 16,528.48 | 495.85 | 17,024.33 |
| 19 | 11,961.47 | 119.61 | 12,081.09 | 17,024.33 | 510.73 | 17,535.06 |
| 20 | 12,081.09 | 120.81 | **$12,201.90** | 17,535.06 | 526.05 | **$18,061.11** |

With a 1% rate of interest, the $10,000 grew to $12,201.90 – the money grew by 22%. With a 3% return, the $10,000 grew to $18,061.11 – a growth of 81%! The difference between getting a 1% return and a 3% return per year becomes the difference between having our money grow by 22% or by 81% over twenty years. And this difference becomes even bigger over a longer period of time – like for example our lives! Most of us will have some money in a savings account for 40, 50, 60 or even 70 years. With $10,000 in our savings accounts for 40 years, at an interest rate of 1% it would become $14,888.64, which is 49% more; at 3%, it would become $32,620.38, which is 226% more. This is a huge difference and a major reason to ensure that we are always saving at the best rate possible.

This example is important because 1% or less is what regular savings or chequing accounts often pay. A better return, such as perhaps 3%, is often possible by looking at savings accounts where the money might be tied up for a little bit longer, but with no more risk than a regular savings account – we will see why shortly at the beginning of the next chapter.

Because interest rates change, it might be that 2% is possible in a regular savings account and that 5% is possible by leaving the money a bit longer; but the principle almost always holds – by seeking out the best return, by perhaps committing to leaving the money for a longer period of time, the return can often be improved dramatically without any additional risk.

If we can get an even higher return than the 3% of our last example, the money will compound even more quickly. Let's see what happens if we compound our money at 7% per year.

| YEAR | BALANCE AT START OF YEAR | RETURN | INTEREST DURING YEAR | NEW TOTAL AT END OF YEAR |
|---|---|---|---|---|
| 1 | 10,000.00 | 7% | 700.00 | 10,700.00 |
| 2 | 10,700.00 | 7% | 749.00 | 11,449.00 |
| 3 | 11,449.00 | 7% | 801.43 | 12,250.43 |
| 4 | 12,250.43 | 7% | 857.53 | 13,107.96 |
| 5 | 13,107.96 | 7% | 917.56 | 14,025.52 |
| 6 | 14,025.52 | 7% | 981.79 | 15,007.30 |
| 7 | 15,007.30 | 7% | 1,050.51 | 16,057.81 |
| 8 | 16,057.81 | 7% | 1,124.05 | 17,181.86 |
| 9 | 17,181.86 | 7% | 1,202.73 | 18,384.59 |
| 10 | 18,384.59 | 7% | 1,286.92 | 19,671.51 |
| 11 | 19,671.51 | 7% | 1,377.01 | 21,048.52 |
| 12 | 21,048.52 | 7% | 1,473.40 | 22,521.92 |
| 13 | 22,521.92 | 7% | 1,576.53 | 24,098.45 |
| 14 | 24,098.45 | 7% | 1,686.89 | 25,785.34 |
| 15 | 25,785.34 | 7% | 1,804.97 | 27,590.32 |
| 16 | 27,590.32 | 7% | 1,931.32 | 29,521.64 |
| 17 | 29,521.64 | 7% | 2,066.51 | 31,588.15 |
| 18 | 31,588.15 | 7% | 2,211.17 | 33,799.32 |
| 19 | 33,799.32 | 7% | 2,365.95 | 36,165.28 |
| 20 | 36,165.28 | 7% | 2,531.57 | $38,696.84 |

**That little difference over one year compounds to a very large difference over many years.** With a 7% annual return, the $10,000 grew to $38,696.84 – a return of 287%. When we were compounding at 1% per year it grew by 22% and when we were compounding at 3% per year it grew by 81%.

We should note that in the 1% and 3% examples we were able to increase our rate of return without taking on extra risk – the difference was purely based on getting a better rate at the bank, by perhaps committing to leaving the money at the bank for a little bit longer. A rate of 7% is often not possible just by tying the money up for longer in the same risk-free way. However, 7% has been possible over the long term with very traditional and socially acceptable investments - investments that governments often even encourage us to make! It is in line with or less than what would have been achieved by investing in the 500 most widely held stocks in the United States (the S&P 500 index) over any 20-year period that ended between 1950 and 2005. The US stock market is a good one to look at because a lot of historical data is available; the return of the UK market or of European markets is very similar, and in some cases even better.

**A great way to save is to save small amounts on a regular basis - the benefits of compounding will again be very noticeable.** For example, if we save $1,000 each year, or $2.74 per day for each day of the year with a 5% return, it would look like this:

| YEAR | BALANCE AT START OF YEAR | INTEREST RATE | INTEREST DURING YEAR | CONTRIBUTION | NEW TOTAL AT END OF YEAR |
|---|---|---|---|---|---|
| 1 | 0.00 | 5% | 0.00 | 1,000.00 | 1,000.00 |
| 2 | 1,000.00 | 5% | 50.00 | 1,000.00 | 2,050.00 |
| 3 | 2,050.00 | 5% | 102.50 | 1,000.00 | 3,152.50 |
| 4 | 3,152.50 | 5% | 157.63 | 1,000.00 | 4,310.13 |
| 5 | 4,310.13 | 5% | 215.51 | 1,000.00 | 5,525.63 |
| 6 | 5,525.63 | 5% | 276.28 | 1,000.00 | 6,801.91 |
| 7 | 6,801.91 | 5% | 340.10 | 1,000.00 | 8,142.01 |
| 8 | 8,142.01 | 5% | 407.10 | 1,000.00 | 9,549.11 |
| 9 | 9,549.11 | 5% | 477.46 | 1,000.00 | 11,026.56 |
| 10 | 11,026.56 | 5% | 551.33 | 1,000.00 | 12,577.89 |
| 11 | 12,577.89 | 5% | 628.89 | 1,000.00 | 14,206.79 |
| 12 | 14,206.79 | 5% | 710.34 | 1,000.00 | 15,917.13 |
| 13 | 15,917.13 | 5% | 795.86 | 1,000.00 | 17,712.98 |
| 14 | 17,712.98 | 5% | 885.65 | 1,000.00 | 19,598.63 |
| 15 | 19,598.63 | 5% | 979.93 | 1,000.00 | 21,578.56 |
| 16 | 21,578.56 | 5% | 1,078.93 | 1,000.00 | 23,657.49 |
| 17 | 23,657.49 | 5% | 1,182.87 | 1,000.00 | 25,840.37 |
| 18 | 25,840.37 | 5% | 1,292.02 | 1,000.00 | 28,132.38 |
| 19 | 28,132.38 | 5% | 1,406.62 | 1,000.00 | 30,539.00 |
| 20 | 30,539.00 | 5% | 1,526.95 | 1,000.00 | **$33,065.95** |

Saving $2.74 per day is not very much – for many of us it might mean saving an expense like a coffee, some sweets, or a pack of cigarettes every day. Nonetheless, over twenty years we will have stored away $20,000 - the $1,000 per year multiplied by the twenty years - and we will have ended up with over $33,000 because of compounding - a nice large number, especially when compared to the $2.74 a day saved.

If we can save $300 per month, which is slightly less than $10 per day on average, the amount that we would end up with is:

| YEAR | BALANCE AT START OF YEAR | INTEREST RATE | INTEREST DURING YEAR | CONTRIBUTION | NEW TOTAL AT END OF YEAR |
|---|---|---|---|---|---|
| 1 | 0 | 5% | 0.00 | 3,600.00 | 3,600.00 |
| 2 | 3,600.00 | 5% | 180.00 | 3,600.00 | 7,380.00 |
| 3 | 7,380.00 | 5% | 369.00 | 3,600.00 | 11,349.00 |
| 4 | 11,349.00 | 5% | 567.45 | 3,600.00 | 15,516.45 |
| 5 | 15,516.45 | 5% | 775.82 | 3,600.00 | 19,892.27 |
| 6 | 19,892.27 | 5% | 994.61 | 3,600.00 | 24,486.89 |
| 7 | 24,486.89 | 5% | 1,224.34 | 3,600.00 | 29,311.23 |
| 8 | 29,311.23 | 5% | 1,465.56 | 3,600.00 | 34,376.79 |
| 9 | 34,376.79 | 5% | 1,718.84 | 3,600.00 | 39,695.63 |
| 10 | 39,695.63 | 5% | 1,984.78 | 3,600.00 | 45,280.41 |
| 11 | 45,280.41 | 5% | 2,264.02 | 3,600.00 | 51,144.43 |
| 12 | 51,144.43 | 5% | 2,557.22 | 3,600.00 | 57,301.66 |
| 13 | 57,301.66 | 5% | 2,865.08 | 3,600.00 | 63,766.74 |
| 14 | 63,766.74 | 5% | 3,188.34 | 3,600.00 | 70,555.08 |
| 15 | 70,555.08 | 5% | 3,527.75 | 3,600.00 | 77,682.83 |
| 16 | 77,682.83 | 5% | 3,884.14 | 3,600.00 | 85,166.97 |
| 17 | 85,166.97 | 5% | 4,258.35 | 3,600.00 | 93,025.32 |
| 18 | 93,025.32 | 5% | 4,651.27 | 3,600.00 | 101,276.58 |
| 19 | 101,276.58 | 5% | 5,063.83 | 3,600.00 | 109,940.41 |
| 20 | 109,940.41 | 5% | 5,497.02 | 3,600.00 | **$119,037.43** |

The small amounts on any given day became very substantial sums of money - better to think about this now rather than later.

Realistically, when we save, we should be able to save money regularly and save more as we get older and as we progress through our careers. Let's look at what happens if we are able to save $7,200 in the first year of a new job (or $600 per month – this is just under $20 per day), and that we can increase this amount by 5% each year. The average return used is again 7%.

| YEAR | BALANCE AT START OF YEAR | INTEREST RATE | INTEREST DURING YEAR | CONTRIBUTION | NEW TOTAL AT END OF YEAR |
|------|--------------------------|---------------|----------------------|--------------|--------------------------|
| 1 | 0 | 7% | 0.00 | 7,200.00 | 7,200.00 |
| 2 | 7,200.00 | 7% | 504.00 | 7,560.00 | 15,264.00 |
| 3 | 15,264.00 | 7% | 1,068.48 | 7,938.00 | 24,270.48 |
| 4 | 24,270.48 | 7% | 1,698.93 | 8,334.90 | 34,304.31 |
| 5 | 34,304.31 | 7% | 2,401.30 | 8,751.65 | 45,457.26 |
| 6 | 45,457.26 | 7% | 3,182.01 | 9,189.23 | 57,828.50 |
| 7 | 57,828.50 | 7% | 4,047.99 | 9,648.69 | 71,525.18 |
| 8 | 71,525.18 | 7% | 5,006.76 | 10,131.12 | 86,663.06 |
| 9 | 86,663.06 | 7% | 6,066.41 | 10,637.68 | 103,367.16 |
| 10 | 103,367.16 | 7% | 7,235.70 | 11,169.56 | 121,772.42 |
| 11 | 121,772.42 | 7% | 8,524.07 | 11,728.04 | 142,024.53 |
| 12 | 142,024.53 | 7% | 9,941.72 | 12,314.44 | 164,280.69 |
| 13 | 164,280.69 | 7% | 11,499.65 | 12,930.17 | 188,710.51 |
| 14 | 188,710.51 | 7% | 13,209.74 | 13,576.67 | 215,496.92 |
| 15 | 215,496.92 | 7% | 15,084.78 | 14,255.51 | 244,837.21 |
| 16 | 244,837.21 | 7% | 17,138.60 | 14,968.28 | 276,944.10 |
| 17 | 276,944.10 | 7% | 19,386.09 | 15,716.70 | 312,046.88 |
| 18 | 312,046.88 | 7% | 21,843.28 | 16,502.53 | 350,392.70 |
| 19 | 350,392.70 | 7% | 24,527.49 | 17,327.66 | 392,247.84 |
| 20 | 392,247.84 | 7% | 27,457.35 | 18,194.04 | 437,899.23 |
| 21 | 437,899.23 | 7% | 30,652.95 | 19,103.74 | 487,655.92 |
| 22 | 487,655.92 | 7% | 34,135.91 | 20,058.93 | 541,850.77 |
| 23 | 541,850.77 | 7% | 37,929.55 | 21,061.88 | 600,842.20 |
| 24 | 600,842.20 | 7% | 42,058.95 | 22,114.97 | 665,016.12 |
| 25 | 665,016.12 | 7% | 46,551.13 | 23,220.72 | 734,787.97 |
| 26 | 734,787.97 | 7% | 51,435.16 | 24,381.76 | 810,604.89 |
| 27 | 810,604.89 | 7% | 56,742.34 | 25,600.84 | 892,948.07 |
| 28 | 892,948.07 | 7% | 62,506.36 | 26,880.89 | 982,335.32 |
| 29 | 982,335.32 | 7% | 68,763.47 | 28,224.93 | 1,079,323.72 |
| 30 | 1,079,323.72 | 7% | 75,552.66 | 29,636.18 | $1,184,512.56 |

After thirty years, we ended up with over one million dollars - a very significant amount!

We could do many more examples like this by playing around with the numbers on a spreadsheet program and a computer. We could gain additional insights by making assumptions regarding our savings, our returns and the number of years that we will be saving. **The key for us however is to get started, and how we should get started will become increasingly clear. The message is certainly clear – compounding is a very powerful way of accumulating savings.**

**The other crucial part of compounding concerns money that we owe. Just as compounding can make amounts that we save grow, compounding can make debts that we owe grow. And because interest rates on debt**

**are almost always higher than interest rates on savings deposits, debts will unfortunately almost always grow faster than savings in our savings account.** Companies that are doing the lending want to make money, but also, for them the risk of not getting repaid is higher when making a loan to us, or to a person in general, than the risk is for us when we deposit money at the bank. When the risk of not getting repaid is higher, so is the return that the lender demands and that the borrower has to pay. The interest rate that we pay on debt is often referred to as the APR (the Annual Percentage Rate), and it is the percentage cost of the debt, including the interest cost plus any other expenses such as administrative expenses or insurance.

The interest rates are particularly high for credit card debt, and these debts can compound very quickly to very large sums. Let's look at $10,000 of credit card debt compounding at 16% for 5 years.

| YEAR | BALANCE AT START OF YEAR | INTEREST RATE | INTEREST DURING YEAR | NEW TOTAL AT END OF YEAR |
|------|--------------------------|---------------|----------------------|--------------------------|
| 1 | 10,000.00 | 16% | 1,600.00 | 11,600.00 |
| 2 | 11,600.00 | 16% | 1,856.00 | 13,456.00 |
| 3 | 13,456.00 | 16% | 2,152.96 | 15,608.96 |
| 4 | 15,608.96 | 16% | 2,497.43 | 18,106.39 |
| 5 | 18,106.39 | 16% | 2,897.02 | $21,003.42 |

**The amount owed has more than doubled in five years without any further spending.** After another five years, this credit card debt would grow to $44,115. If more were spent in the meantime, the debt would grow even more quickly!

**Any amount left on a credit card will grow very quickly, and this is a dangerous way of letting our debts get worse and worse. It can lead to big problems**, especially if the debt grows while the purchased item becomes worthless. A week after the purchase, the only thing left is the growing debt. Even if the debt is eventually paid off, the amount that has to be paid back can be a lot larger than the amount spent.

To further illustrate this, we can think of what an item would actually cost if we do not pay for it right away. A CD bought on a credit card for $15, with a card that is not paid off for five years (again with a credit card interest rate of 16%), actually costs $31.51 in five years.

| YEAR | BALANCE AT START OF YEAR | INTEREST RATE | INTEREST DURING YEAR | NEW TOTAL AT END OF YEAR |
|---|---|---|---|---|
| 1 | 15.00 | 16% | 2.40 | 17.40 |
| 2 | 17.40 | 16% | 2.78 | 20.18 |
| 3 | 20.18 | 16% | 3.23 | 23.41 |
| 4 | 23.41 | 16% | 3.75 | 27.16 |
| 5 | 27.16 | 16% | 4.35 | **$31.51** |

The CD ultimately cost slightly more than twice the original price because of the interest and the effect of compounding. We have to ask ourselves whether a CD is worth paying $31.51 for in five years' time, before making a purchase on this basis. It might be better to wait until we have the money in hand! Also, wouldn't it be nicer to see $15 compound in our savings account to a larger sum, instead of watching our debt balloon as it will with such high interest rates?

Even if we make the interest payments regularly, the cost of this CD will still be much higher than the purchase price. How much higher depends on how long we pay interest for – in theory if we keep the debt outstanding for a long period of time, the amount paid will be much much higher.

**We can think of debt as the mirror image of saving - the amount still grows but now it is money that we owe that is growing, not money that we have that is growing. The effects of compounding are just as important, if not more so because of the higher interest rates. Paying off credit card debt or other high interest rate debt is always a priority because the debt will grow so quickly.**

In conclusion, it is clear that by harnessing the power of compounding for our savings, we can make our savings grow in a fantastic way. **Compounding is probably the most important concept of any savings plan – we will simply not be able to grow our money effectively or save for large purchases without making use of compounding.** On the other hand, outstanding debt, particularly at high interest rates, typically grows even more quickly, and this can become very dangerous. We want our assets to grow while we sleep and while a return is being generated for us. We certainly do not want our debts to accumulate while we sleep, or even lose sleep over our finances.

KEY QUESTIONS THAT WE CAN ANSWER AFTER READING THIS CHAPTER
(CHECK THAT YOU CAN):

1.  WHAT IS COMPOUNDING?
2.  DOES THE MONEY GROW, OR GROW FASTER AND FASTER WITH COMPOUNDING?
3.  HOW DO SMALL SAVED AMOUNTS ACCUMULATE TO LARGER AMOUNTS?
4.  IS STARTING AS SOON AS POSSIBLE IMPORTANT?
5.  WHAT AFFECTS THE AMOUNT OF MONEY THAT WE COMPOUND TO?
6.  CAN A SMALL DIFFERENCE IN THE RETURN PER YEAR, COMPOUND TO A LARGE DIFFERENCE OVER MANY YEARS?
7.  WHY IS CREDIT CARD DEBT SUCH A BAD IDEA?
8.  HOW DOES DEBT COMPOUND AND WHAT DOES THAT MEAN FOR THINGS THAT WE BUY ON CREDIT CARDS?

(THE ANSWERS CAN BE EASILY FOUND IN THIS CHAPTER)

# Chapter II

# DEBT, EQUITY AND FINANCIAL MARKETS

Compounding our money with a return over a longer period is the key to accumulating larger sums, but what is it that allows our money to receive a return, and what determines whether this return will be good or bad? This is what we are going to look at in this section. This will also help us understand why banks give us interest in the first place, and why they do not run out of money when they pay interest on all of the money that is deposited with them.

**As savers and investors, a key way for us to compound our money is by directly or indirectly making our money available to *users of capital*. Users of capital can be companies or governments, who are looking for money to undertake projects or to buy something.** If the user of capital that we make our money available to is willing and able to pay a return for having the money, we as providers will collect a return and compound our money. With this structure, both sides benefit – we get a return for having made the money available, and the user of capital has the money to undertake what they wanted to. **In other words, we as savers can be *providers of capital*, and compound our money because a user of capital is paying to have access to it.**

When we deposit money at the bank, we are effectively lending it to the bank. Banks will receive our money, and the money of many other savers, and lend it out in large quantities to users of capital. The bank is the intermediary between savers and users of capital in this case. The users of capital that the bank lends the money to will pay the bank for having access to the money - from this return that the bank receives, it pays interest to us. The bank also keeps a little bit for themselves (and this is one of the main ways that banks make money).

**How the bank lends the money out in order to get the return, determines the return the bank gets and what they can then pay to us.** If the bank is able to lend the money out for a longer period of time, the bank should be able to earn a higher return and pay a higher return to us. This is because longer-term interest rates tend to be higher than short-term interest rates. Since we often have some money at the bank for longer periods of time anyway, we can get this higher return simply by telling the bank ahead of time that the money will be there for this longer period of time.

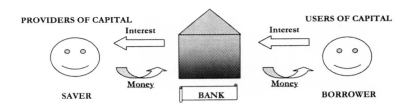

Lending money involves *debt* – an obligation for a borrower to repay a certain amount of money known as the *principal* to the lender. We can lend money, and make use of a debt type relationship, by lending money to the bank via our savings account as above (with the bank then lending it on for a return). We can also, as we shall see in more detail later, lend money directly, or via a fund, to large users of capital such as companies and governments who offer a return in the form of interest to savers and investors based on the revenues they receive – companies from their business activities, and governments mainly by collecting taxes. Based on what the companies and governments pay, savers and investors can compound their money. **Lending money to users of capital (or investing in debt) is the first main way that we can compound our money. How quickly it grows will be determined by the return that the borrower is willing and able to pay.**

We often just think of debt as money that we owe, where we are the user of capital, but we need to bear in mind that on the other side of that debt is a lender who is compounding their money and making it grow! **When we have money as savers, we can make money available to others through debt structures and be the *lender* as opposed to the *borrower*.** When we do this, we will be the ones collecting the interest and growing our money.

**Investors often lend money to *large users* of capital (like companies or governments) by buying *bonds*.** A purchaser of a bond pays a certain amount to buy the bond, and this is the amount that the investor has effectively lent to the user of capital. The purchaser of the bond (the bondholder) typically receives interest periodically until the bond (and therefore the loan) ends, at which point the purchaser of the bond expects to receive the principal of the loan back (at maturity). We will discuss bonds in more detail when we talk about investments.

**Debt is the first way that providers and users of capital interact, and the first way that we can compound our money.**

**The other main way for us to compound our money is through *ownership* or *equity*** – by becoming owners or part-owners of companies. Our return in this case will depend greatly on how the companies do. The discussion of compounding our money via ownership is relevant for investing in companies, because companies have this second way of raising money. Many institutions can raise money in the form of debt, whereas companies can raise money in the form of debt *and* equity. The government, for example, as the institution that represents the people of a country, can borrow, and therefore raise money via debt, but it cannot have owners that buy its equity.

The most common way for savers and investors to compound their money via ownership in companies is through stocks or shares, which are pieces of the equity of a company that are listed on a stock exchange. Savers and investors can buy a stock and thereby become owners of a small slice of the equity of a company. All of the shareholders together own the entire company, and each share of *common* stock as it is also known, is identical to every other share of common stock. Before we speak specifically about stocks and the stock market, let's look at how a company is financed in principle, and how the returns for the providers of capital vary depending on the performance of this hypothetical company.

Let's take an example of a company that is created by someone who makes $50,000 available as equity and invests it as an owner in a restaurant. In other words, this money is provided by a provider of capital in the form of equity. He then borrows $50,000 from a neighbour at an interest rate of 7% per year – this money is provided in the form of debt. The $100,000 total is used to buy a restaurant. We can show the value of the assets of the company on the left side, and its funding from the providers of capital on the right side in what is known as a *Balance Sheet*.

| RESTAURANT 100,000 | DEBT 50,000 |
| | EQUITY 50,000 |

We can then look at how the returns to the equity and debt vary depending on what happens with this company/restaurant. Let's say that in the first year of business, the restaurant earns $8,000 after all expenses. How much the company makes – its profit or net income – is calculated using an *Income Statement* as shown below.

| REVENUE/SALES | $100,000 |
|---|---|
| **Less Expenses** | |
| Cost of Food | 20,000 |
| Salaries | 50,000 |
| Rent | 6,000 |
| Insurance | 1,650 |
| Interest Expense (7%) | 3,500 |
| Other Expenses | 6,850 |
| *Total Expenses* | *88,000* |
| **Pretax Profit** | 12,000 |
| Taxes | 4,000 |
| | |
| **NET INCOME** | **$8,000** |

The return for the debtholder (the provider of capital in the form of debt) is 7% as was agreed when the money was borrowed.

The return to the provider of capital through equity – the equityholder or owner – is determined by the net income, which is what is left over after all expenses have been paid – in this case $8,000. In this case, on a percentage basis the return is 16% – a return of $8,000 for an investment of $50,000. It could have been less, it could have been more, but in this case it was $8,000 for an investment of $50,000, or 16%. **As we can see, the equityholder's return was not fixed at the time the money was provided – it was determined by how the company performed in that year.** The equityholder could receive this return in the form of a cash dividend, which means that it would be paid out in cash, or the $8,000 could be kept within the company, in which case the value of his/her equity stake would rise by $8,000. The company could also do a combination of the two, for example, pay out $4,000 and keep $4,000 within the company. In any case the return would add up to 16% typically.

Let's assume that the company keeps the $8,000 of net income inside the company, in this case the new balance sheet looks like this:

| RESTAURANT 108,000 | **DEBT** 50,000 |
| | **EQUITY** 58,000 |

Let's assume that in the next year, the company has sales of $120,000 and the income statement looks as follows.

| **REVENUE/SALES** | $120,000 |
|---|---|
| **Less Expenses** | |
| Cost of Food | 25,000 |
| Salaries | 52,500 |
| Rent | 6,500 |
| Insurance | 1,650 |
| Interest Expense (7%) | 3,500 |
| Other Expenses | 6,850 |
| *Total Expenses* | *96,000* |
| **Pretax Profit** | 24,000 |
| Taxes | 8,000 |
| | |
| **NET INCOME** | **$16,000** |

The company made $16,000, and the return on equity is therefore $16,000 on equity capital that is now $58,000 – a return for the equityholder of 28%. The return to the equityholder changed because of the higher net income. The return to the debtholder stays at 7%; it has not increased with the better performance of the company in the second year.

The fact that the return to the debtholder is less variable is confirmed by the structure of the Income Statement. The interest expense, which determines the return of the debtholder, is subtracted from the revenues before we get to the net income that is left for the equityholders. In other words, debtholders get their money before equityholders, and it is usually a fixed amount amount or a fixed percentage. Equityholders get what is left over, but benefit more if the company does well.

Let's assume that the money the company made in the second year is again kept inside the company so that the equity grows by $16,000; the equity capital is now $74,000 ($58,000 + $16,000).

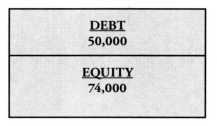

Let's see what happens to the return for the providers of capital via debt and equity when the value of the assets changes dramatically. In the third year, let's assume that the only thing that happens is that the value of the restaurant doubles, because the value of the land that the restaurant sits on appreciates dramatically. We will assume that the company made just enough revenues to cover its expenses, and that the net income or net profit was zero.

If the value of the restaurant rises, the two sides of the <u>Balance</u> Sheet still have to <u>balance</u>, and it is the value of the equity (the ownership part) on the right side of the sheet that will rise to ensure that the balanced relationship still holds. The debt (the lending part) will not increase – the company will not owe more money just because it is worth more. Furthermore, the debt has a fixed return and both the user and the provider of capital understand that.

<table>
<tr>
<td rowspan="2" align="center"><u>RESTAURANT</u><br>248,000</td>
<td align="center"><u>DEBT</u><br>50,000</td>
</tr>
<tr>
<td align="center"><u>EQUITY</u><br>198,000</td>
</tr>
</table>

The owner's equity went from $74,000 to $198,000 – his return on paper is $124,000 - a percentage return of 168% ($124,000/$74,000 x 100%). The return to the debtholder stays at 7%. Again, the equity return is much more variable and depends much more on what is happening with the company.

Let's assume that in the fourth year, the only thing that happens is that the value of the restaurant declines by 60%, from $248,000 to $100,000, because of a downturn in the real estate market. Again it will be the owner's equity that changes to ensure that the two sides balance. It is the equity that takes the hit when the value of the company declines, just as it was the equity that benefited when the value of the company rose.

| RESTAURANT 100,000 | DEBT 50,000 |
| | EQUITY 50,000 |

The return for the debtholder will still be 7%. The return to the equityholder, whose equity has now gone from $198,000 to $50,000, is the loss of equity of $148,000 divided by his investment of $198,000, which gives a return of -75%.

Over the four years, the returns for the equityholder of the restaurant were 16% in year 1, 28% in year 2, 168% in year 3 and – 75% in year 4. The return to the debtholder stayed constant at 7% over the four years. The return for the bondholder in this example would typically only change if the company is no longer able to generate enough revenues to pay the interest on the debt, which will take place only if the company runs into financial difficulties – otherwise the return for the debtholder remains constant and as initially agreed. **Clearly the return for the equityholder depended very much on how the company performed and how the value of its assets changed.**

Interestingly, in the last two examples, when the value of the restaurant went up and down, the percentage return to the equityholder was higher than the percentage change in the value of the restaurant. When the value of the restaurant went up by 100%, the owner's stake increased by 168%. When the value of the restaurant fell by 60%, the equity fell by 75%. **The reason that the percentage change in the equity was greater than the percentage change in the value of the asset is because the equityholder's return was magnified by *leverage*.** The word leverage comes from the word lever, which is a mechanical tool that magnifies a given force to have a greater impact. Leverage played a role here because the equityholder used a certain amount of money and augmented it with debt to have a magnified financial impact. When the value of the asset rises on the left side, the debt on the right does not really change, so the equity has to change more on a percentage basis to make up for this. For example, if we have $50 and borrow another $50 to purchase something worth $100, if the item rises quickly in value by 20% to $120, the amount borrowed would still be $50 and our stake (the equity) would have gone from $50 to $70 ($120 - $50); our return as owners (on the equity) would be 40% [($70–$50)/$50 x 100%] because of leverage, not the 20% that the asset rose in value.

> **Because leverage magnifies our returns, using leverage increases risk. If the item goes up in value, we have a magnified better return, but if the item drops in value, we have a magnified worse return.**
>
> **The most common and significant use of leverage for most of us is for the purchase of a home.** The debt in this case is called a mortgage. Crucially, when we use debt or leverage to buy a home, the interest rates are usually the lowest rates that we can get – a real estate investment is an asset that tends to retain its value well, there is an approval process for mortgages, and the lender knows where the asset is. In other words, the risk for the mortgage lender is much lower; therefore the lender can make the interest rate much lower. Mortgage interest rates tend to be lower than all other personal interest rates, and are certainly much lower than credit card interest rates. Having said that, most mortgages allow the lender to take the property if we repeatedly fail to make our payments, therefore it is essential that we can afford the debt. If we can make the interest payments, and we want to borrow, then borrowing against our home is usually the best way to reduce our interest costs; whereas borrowing on a credit card is by far the worst.
>
> The key to having debt and leverage is to be prudent, to ensure that the cost of debt is as low as possible, and to ensure that we are not magnifying a return through leverage that is likely to end up being very negative.

Let's go back to our hypothetical company – the restaurant. As we saw, the returns to the equityholders were much more variable than the returns to the debtholders – in other words, because equity depends much more on what is happening with the company, the returns to equity are much more variable than those for the investors in the debt.

Debt and equityholders provide the initial capital to the company as we saw, and the company uses its net income and its cash flows from the business to invest and grow over time. If at some point the investments that the company has to make require more money than these cash flows provide, the company might need to take in additional capital, and this capital will come from debt and/or equity investors again. For example, to fund the expansion, the owner might find an outside investor, who might invest $50,000 of cash as equity. The balance sheet would then look like this:

| Restaurant: | 100,000 | Equity of Original Owner: 50,000 |
|---|---|---|
| Cash: | 50,000 | Equity of Outside Investor: 50,000 |
| | | Debt: 50,000 |
| Total Assets | $150,000 | Total Equity & Debt    $150,000 |

With the additional $50,000 in cash, the assets increase from $100,000 to $150,000 - the company now has an additional $50,000 to spend on expanding. The assets on the left side still balance with the sources of funding on the right side. When a company raises money through equity as above, the fact that the equity does not require interest payments is an advantage, particularly for a small company that is starting out, and probably not making a lot of money. The main disadvantage for the original owner in raising money via equity is that he/she now shares the equity of the company with another equity investor - he/she will have to share the return of the company with the new investor; in this case, both would receive 50% of the return that the business generates.

Instead of taking on an outside equity investor, the owner could have decided to raise the same amount of money through debt:

| Restaurant: | 150,000 | Equity of Original Owner: | 50,000 |
|---|---|---|---|
| Cash: | 50,000 | Debt: | 100,000 |
| Total Assets | $150,000 | Total Equity & Debt | $150,000 |

The left side would go up by the $50,000 of cash that was raised, and the debt on the right side would increase by $50,000 to reflect the additional debt. By using debt, the owner would have increased the leverage, and would have to pay interest on the debt, but after that, as the sole equityholder, he/she would continue to get all of the income and appreciation.

As companies grow, they typically go through multiple rounds of financing like this where they take on additional equity or debt capital. The equity is referred to as private equity and the investment often comes from professional private equity investors – more on this in the next chapter. The debt investment often comes from banks and sometimes other financial institutions.

If over time the company is successful and it grows, the value of the company's assets and therefore also the value of the equity and debt will become very large (as per the Balance Sheet). In order for the equity and debtholders not to own very large pieces of debt and equity that can not be easily sold or diversified, and also to allow the company to raise additional capital if necessary more easily, it might be beneficial for the company to slice its debt and/or equity into many smaller pieces. Instead of having one or two large pieces of debt or equity, there could be hundreds or even thousands of pieces of debt and/or equity that many providers of capital could invest in.

**This is exactly what happens, and these smaller slices of debt are known as *bonds*.** If a user of capital decides to borrow a large amount such as $10,000,000 using bonds, the user could sell 10,000 bonds, each valued at $1,000 (10,000 x $1,000 = $10,000,000) to raise the money. A set of conditions would describe how the company expects to repay each bond, and these conditions will be the same for each bond of that type - for example, each bond might pay a 7% interest coupon annually and the amount might be repaid in five years when the bond matures. Investors will buy the bonds on the expectation that these are the terms that they will receive. Each bond investor will own a part of the overall debt of that user of capital, and each bond investor has effectively lent money to the user of capital.

**When a company splits its equity into many smaller slices that are made available to the public, it does so via its *initial public offering (IPO)*, where equity shares are offered to the public for the first time.** After the *IPO*, the company is said to be a *public company* and the shares have been *listed*. The small slices of equity that providers of capital can invest in are known as *shares* or *stocks*, and they can be bought (and sold) on a *stock exchange*. Each buyer of a stock becomes a part owner of the company. The shares that are listed might come from the owner who might sell some shares, and/or from the company who could issue new shares to raise capital. For example, initially a company's market value might look like this:

| Company: | $10,000,000 | Equity (Private): | 5,000,000 |
|---|---|---|---|
| | | Debt: | 5,000,000 |
| | | | $10,000,000 |

If this company wants to become public and list many smaller shares, they have to choose a share price, which multiplied by the number of shares will be equal to the value of the equity. For example, if the company decides to set an initial price for each share of $50, in this example, the number of shares will be $5,000,000/$50, or 100,000 shares.

Let's say that at the initial public offering, the owner decides to sell 10% of his stake or 10,000 shares, and that the company has also decided to create 10,000 new shares to sell to the market to raise money for the company. After the IPO, the new picture will look like this:

| Company: | $10,500,000 | Equity (Public): | |
|---|---|---|---|
| | | - Existing Owner: | 4,500,000 |
| | | - Outside Owners | 1,000,000 |
| | | Debt: | 5,000,000 |
| | | | $10,500,000 |

The existing owner now owns 100,000 − 10,000 = 90,000 shares, which is equivalent to $4,500,000 (90,000 x $50) of equity. New shareholders bought the 10,000 shares that the owner sold, and the 10,000 shares that were sold by the company to the market to raise money; the total equity owned by outside owners is therefore 20,000 shares or $1,000,000 (20,000 x $50). Because 10,000 new shares were sold to raise money, the value of the company also increased by $500,000 (10,000 x $50).

**Once shares are listed on the stock exchange, they can be bought and sold readily by outside investors like you or me or bigger institutional investors.** The shares can be bought or sold by going to our bank or a broker or via the Internet. Each buyer of a share becomes a part owner of the company, and is entitled to certain rights including the opportunity to vote for management, receive dividends from the company's income and participate in the change in value of the equity. The return that a shareholder in a public company receives will depend greatly on how the company performs and its net income as in the previous examples, and it will also depend on how investors value the equity based on their view of the company's future – more on this in the next chapter.

**Many large companies split their debt and equity into many smaller slices, and many other users of capital such as governments also split their debt into many smaller slices – ultimately there are literally millions of different pieces of equity and debt available.** There are also millions of providers of capital looking for a return – individuals, fund and pension managers, banks and other financial institutions. Due to the large number of users and providers of capital, **a market, or a financial market, for the equity and the debt to trade in makes a lot of sense.** In the financial market, the many users of capital that require funds to undertake projects, or to grow, can interact with savers and investors who provide capital looking for a return. In fact, because there are so many different users and providers of capital with different needs and preferences, there is more than one financial market, and also there are different terms used to describe different areas of the financial markets. There are the stock and the bond markets of course - where providers of capital make funds available as owners or lenders, by investing in the slices of the equity and debt of users of capital respectively. Investors also often refer to the money market, which is a financial market for short-term debt of one year or less, and the capital market – the market for transactions of over one year, which would include the stock market. (Sometimes the terms are used a little loosely, and the term capital market is often used to refer to the entire financial market).

**Because of the access to many providers of capital, a financial market allows users of capital to raise much larger sums than they could anywhere else.** This access to capital is essential for large users of capital as it allows large projects that require significant sums of money to be undertaken – it can allow large companies to be financed, governments to build motorway systems, companies to raise additional funds for medical research, and even groups of homeowners to borrow for their home purchases. Also, in a financial market, if a provider of capital wants their money back, the user of capital does not have to repay it - the provider of capital can get their money back by selling the investment to another provider of capital, and the user still has access to the funds. This is a big advantage for users of capital and is known as permanency of capital.

**For providers of capital, including savers, financial markets also offer a lot of benefits:**

- *Choice* – providers of capital have access to many different investments to choose from to try and get a return because of the many different users of capital that go there. Each provider of capital can also split his money among numerous investments to diversify;
- *Centralisation* – even if the actual users of capital are not conducting their business in one place, the investments are available in one place. This makes investing much easier;
- *Liquidity* – because there are many market participants, buying and selling without the price moving a lot is much easier in a financial market. Providers of capital can more easily pull out of an investment by selling it to someone else than would otherwise be possible.

**All providers of capital come to the financial market seeking a return in order to reap the benefits of compounding, and this return can only be earned if the party that the money is given to – the user of capital - can deliver a return.** Many users of capital are able to do this and that is why most stock and bond markets have offered a positive return over the long term. But not every user of capital is able to deliver a return, and the returns between different users of capital also vary. For us as savers and investors, figuring out the good places to put the money in order to earn a return is the challenge in making investments. When we lend money to stable companies or developed-country governments, by becoming debtholders or bondholders, we can be fairly certain that these entities can generate enough revenues to pay interest to us for making the money available. When investing in the equity of companies, it is more difficult to know which companies will be successful and which will not - many companies fail and are not able to earn a return for investors.

**When a company fails, the money that providers of capital made available was in a way wasted since the company obviously did not provide a return for investors, but that is not the only problem.** The company was also probably not successful in providing a product or service to society at the right price, and it was not successful in creating jobs over the long term. Being able to offer a good return usually goes hand in hand with creating something that society values and is willing to pay for - for example a new product in the field of medicine or a service that improves the quality of life. Companies that can do this at the right price should be the ones that earn profits and returns for investors. As a provider of capital, focusing on getting a return is therefore incredibly important, firstly because the returns can compound to very large sums over time, and secondly because the parties that are able to provide a return are usually the ones that can deliver things that society values, and they are usually the ones that can create jobs. These parties in fact require access to funding, and providers of capital play a crucial role by giving it to them.

**One of the key functions of the financial markets is to try and figure out which users of capital will be able to deliver a return, and which users of capital are therefore deserving of capital from investors. This will be based on their ability to generate revenues, the need for their product or service, the business plan, their strategy, the quality of their management among other factors**. Hundreds and thousands of portfolio managers and analysts try to figure out which investments should be invested in by analysing the above factors.

And this is the question that we always have to ask ourselves when making investments; we will look at this in more detail in the next chapter.

**In summary, we as savers and investors have two key ways of interacting with users of capital – through debt and equity. Each of these two ways has distinct characteristics, and financial markets play a key role in facilitating this interaction. Financial markets allow many savers and investors (providers of capital) to invest and seek a return, and allow many users of capital such as companies and governments to find capital to undertake projects and to grow their businesses. Because of their importance, financial markets are one of the main building blocks of our entire economic system and ultimately our society. Countries with strong, healthy, fair, and well-developed financial markets are able to provide a higher standard of living for residents by allowing providers of capital to compound their savings, and by allowing users of capital to build businesses, fund innovation, create jobs and deliver the best products and services.**

### KEY QUESTIONS THAT WE CAN ANSWER AFTER READING THIS CHAPTER (CHECK THAT YOU CAN):

1. WHAT IMPACTS THE INTEREST RATE THAT BANKS PAY TO US WHEN WE DEPOSIT OUR MONEY THERE?
2. WHAT ARE THE TWO MAIN WAYS IN WHICH WE CAN MAKE MONEY AVAILABLE TO USERS OF CAPITAL?
3. WHAT IS A BALANCE SHEET?
4. WHO CAN SAVERS MAKE THEIR MONEY AVAILABLE TO IN ORDER TO COMPOUND RETURNS?
5. WHAT IS AN INCOME STATEMENT?
6. DO DEBTHOLDERS OR EQUITYHOLDERS GET PAID FIRST?
7. IS THE RETURN TO AN EQUITY INVESTOR MUCH MORE VARIABLE?
8. WHAT IS LEVERAGE AND HOW DOES IT IMPACT RETURNS?
9. WHEN IS LEVERAGE DEFINITELY A BAD IDEA?
10. WHAT DO USERS OF CAPITAL DO WHEN THEIR EQUITY AND DEBT GET VERY LARGE?
11. WHAT ARE SMALLER SLICES OF DEBT KNOWN AS?
12. WHAT ARE THE SMALLER SLICES OF EQUITY KNOWN AS?
13. WHAT IS AN INITIAL PUBLIC OFFERING (IPO)?
14. WHAT IS A FINANCIAL MARKET AND WHAT ARE THE BENEFITS TO PROVIDERS AND USERS OF CAPITAL?
15. WHY IS TRYING TO GET A RETURN IN THE FINANCIAL MARKETS SO IMPORTANT?
16. WHY ARE WELL-FUNCTIONING FINANCIAL MARKETS IMPORTANT?

(THE ANSWERS CAN BE EASILY FOUND IN THIS CHAPTER)

# Chapter III

# INVESTMENTS

**Investments are where we as savers and investors put our money to gain a return – they are the tools that make our money grow.** Two key investments involve providing money to users of capital in the form of debt and equity as we saw - in this chapter we are going to look at these investments in more detail. We are also going to discuss other investments that we as savers can consider.

## 1.   DEBT AND BONDS (FIXED INCOME INVESTMENTS)

**As we saw, the first way for us to compound our money is through *debt investments* – by lending it to users of capital such as governments or companies.** Debt investments are also known as fixed income investments because they tend to pay a fixed income periodically, for example a fixed interest rate or a fixed *coupon*.

**There are many different fixed income investments available.** Fixed income securities include short-term debt such as treasury bills in the US, bonds, mortgage-backed securities, gilts (in the UK) and many other loans that have been split into smaller pieces that then trade in the financial market.

**The specific name for each of the different instruments depends on the issuer and for how long the investor makes the money available for (the maturity of the debt). Although they come with different names, the investments are similar in that they are <u>loans</u>, and that the main issuers are the same - they are:**

- *Governments* that issue *government bonds* and other government debt in order to receive large sums of money in order to undertake major projects like building highways. They usually pay the regular interest on these bonds by using money received from taxes. Federal, state and local governments can issue bonds; in the United States, bonds issued by the state or local government are known as municipal bonds;
- *Companies* that issue *corporate bonds*, which typically pay a coupon based on the company's revenues. Corporate bonds appear as debt on a company's balance sheet;
- *Mortgage Associations/Companies* that issue *mortgage-backed securities*. These institutions hold the mortgages of homeowners and can package them and sell them to savers who receive a return based on the interest paid by the homeowners. Some of these mortgage-backed securities are even guaranteed by the mortgage association (for example the Government National Mortgage Association or GNMA in the United States); in other cases the bonds are often very highly rated (low risk) because of a country's legal framework and the lending criteria that are used (for example in Denmark).

**Because fixed income securities are often just certificates that allow the owner to receive a coupon periodically, a 'bond' can be created anywhere where someone wants to borrow money, and where there is a regular income to pay a coupon.** New types of bonds are created all the time depending on the needs of borrowers, and the purchasing interest of providers of capital. For example, a musician who receives royalties on his/her already released music (regular income) might wish to have one large upfront payment (loan) instead of receiving royalty payments each year. The musician could sell bonds to receive a large sum of money upfront, and then use the money coming in from the music royalties to pay the interest or coupon. This is what David Bowie did when he sold bonds called 'Pullman Bonds' which are named after the inventor David Pullman.

**The maturity of fixed income securities - the length of time over which the money is lent for – can vary from overnight to twenty or more years.**

**The market for short-term debt is known as the money market** and it includes government debt of less than one-year maturity (Treasury Bills in the US), which, because of their short maturity tend to be considered safer and therefore have a lower rate of interest. **The market for longer-term debt of over one year is part of the capital market.** For how long, and therefore where a user of capital will borrow depends on why the money is needed. Longer-term projects like highway construction will require longer-term debt. Short term financing for meeting a temporary cash shortfall will require short-term debt.

**The longer the maturity of the bond, i.e. the longer the money is lent for, the higher the return usually, and there are different theories to explain why this is typically the case.** One theory highlights that shorter-term debt is more liquid (it can be bought and sold more easily without the price moving a lot), so that longer-term debt has to offer a higher return to compensate. Another states that demand is greater for short-term debt, and therefore longer-term debt has to offer a higher return to make it attractive. Another theory, the expectations theory, states that longer-term interest rates reflect the expectation of where shorter-term interest rates will go, and that future short-term rates are generally expected to rise. The bottom line is that longer-term interest rates tend to be higher than shorter-term interest rates, which is why we can also often capture a better interest rate on our money at the bank when we commit to leaving it there for longer - the bank has more options as to what it can do with the money and they can theoretically lend the money out in the longer-term debt market to get a better return, and pay a better return to us.

**Fixed income instruments including bonds can be created in many situations, also there are many different issuers (borrowers), and furthermore one issuer can have many fixed income instruments outstanding.** The result is that there are many many fixed income investments and bonds in existence. Because of this, most of these investments trade via computers and telephones instead of on physical exchanges (as is often the case for stocks). A financial market like this, without a physical exchange, is known as an *over-the-counter (OTC) market*.

**A purchaser of a bond pays a certain sum of money that is effectively lent to the user of capital,** and the purchaser will expect to receive coupon payments usually once or twice per year, and will expect to receive the principal back at maturity. The amount of the coupons and the principal that the investor receives define the return that the provider of capital receives and the amount the user of capital pays. The return of a fixed income investment is also known as its *yield*.

If an investor can buy a one-year bond that pays $1,000 in one year for $900 today, then first of all he would have lent $900 to the user of capital, and the user of capital would be expected to repay $1,000 in one year. The expected return or yield for the investor would be the $100 return (to $1,000 from $900) divided by the investment of $900, expressed as a percentage – this is 11.11% (100/900 x 100%). If an investor paid $1,000 for a one-year bond that in one year paid a coupon of $50, and in one year also repaid the principal of $1,000, then the return or yield would be 5%. If he bought a two-year bond for $1,000 that paid a coupon of $60 each year and that was expected to repay the principal after two years, then the yield for this bond would be 6%.

Some short-term debt fixed income securities are issued at a discount to the principal value or *face value* that will be repaid at maturity, and the return is provided that way. For example the investment might be bought at 99 and it might mature at 100, thereby providing a return of 1.01% over that time period.

**The higher the risk of the debt, the higher the yield or return needs to be in order to make it attractive to investors.** Debt that is issued by the governments of developed countries like the United States, the United Kingdom and most European countries, is considered risk-free and is the lowest risk and lowest expected return, or yield, debt in each country. These governments could theoretically default on their debt, but they are considered to be the last ones that would default, and the risk is considered so small that the debt is considered risk-free. The debt of all other issuers has to provide a slightly higher return to compensate investors for the risk of potentially not receiving the interest or the principal back. For very stable companies this additional return is small – for very risky issuers, it will be much higher.

To describe the riskiness of a bond, rating agencies assign ratings to many fixed income securities including all well-known publicly traded bonds. Two main rating agencies are Moody's and Standard & Poor's and their rating scales are shown below:

| MOODY'S | | STANDARD & POOR'S | |
|---|---|---|---|
| Aaa | Highest Quality | AAA | |
| Aa | Just below best | AA | INVESTMENT GRADE |
| A | High medium grade | A | |
| Baa | Economic Conditions impact ability to repay | BBB | |
| Ba | Speculative bonds Junk Bonds | BB | |
| Ba | | BB | |
| B | | B | NON-INVESTMENT GRADE |
| Caa | Susceptible to Default | CCC | |
| C | Lowest Quality In or close to Default | CC | |
| | | C | |
| | In Default | D | |

*Source: Moody's/Standard & Poor's*

Government bonds in developed countries typically have Aaa/AAA ratings. High quality corporations often have Aa/AA or A/A ratings. When companies issue numerous bonds, some of which get repaid before others, it is possible for the same company to have bonds outstanding with different ratings, depending on which get repaid first.

The rating of a company's debt affects the yield or return on the debt that the investor expects, and on the other hand the cost of the debt for the borrower. If a company issues debt with a poor debt rating, it means that they will have to pay a higher interest rate on that debt each year, which reduces their net income; having a good debt rating is therefore advantageous for issuers of debt – it keeps their interest costs lower.

If the existing debt of a borrower is seen to be more risky, the rating agencies might downgrade the debt. When debt becomes more risky, it means that the price of the debt will fall - it is less valuable given the higher uncertainty. Simultaneously, the yield will rise to reflect the higher risk. Because the coupons that a bond pays are usually fixed at the outset, the expected coupon payments are assumed to remain the same.

For example, a bond is expected to pay a $50 coupon for five years and then repay the principal or face value of $1,000 in the fifth year. If this bond is bought *at par* for $1,000, then it is currently yielding, or providing a return of 5% per year ($50/$1,000). If this bond becomes more risky, its price will fall. The annual coupon payments would still be expected to be $50, and the yield or expected return would rise. For example, if the price fell to $900, the $50 coupons would now provide a yield that is greater than 5%, reflecting the higher risk. For someone that already held the bond, the price would have fallen (although he would still be expecting the same coupons) so the fact that the yield went up is bad. For someone that is thinking about buying the bond, he/she can now buy the bond for $900 and get a better yield (with a higher risk) by receiving the $50 coupons. For the issuer whose debt has been downgraded, the return or yield that the issuer has to pay on future debt issues would also most likely have risen, meaning that it has become more expensive for them to borrow.

**Investing involves paying for something today, to receive cash flows in the future. Knowing what the future cash flows are, can allow us to calculate the value of the investment today. We can use this concept to think about the value of bonds.** Importantly, receiving a cash flow in the future is not as good as receiving the same cash flow today. If we receive the cash flow today, we can earn a return and make more out of that money. For example, with a return of 5%, $100 received today, would become $105 in one year. Getting $100 today is better than getting $100 in one year – getting $100 today is equivalent to getting $105 in one year in this example.

In order to go from the $100 (the present value) to the $105 (the future value), we multiplied by [1+ interest rate] just like we did when we were compounding our returns in the first chapter. In order to go from the *future value* to the *present value*, we would do the opposite of multiplying by [1 + interest rate], which means *dividing* by [1 + interest rate]. A cash flow of $400, if the correct interest rate was 12%, would be worth $400/[1+12%] = $357.14 to us today. (The two choices are equivalent since $357.14 would become $400 if we receive 12% interest on that money for one year).

The fact that we can say that a certain cash flow in the future is equivalent to getting a certain cash flow today, allows us to value bonds or determine their yields. Bonds are really just a series of future cash flows, and if we can bring these cash flows back to today, we can value the bond. Bringing a future value back to its value today is known as *discounting*. The interest rate used to bring the future cash flows back to today is also known as the *required rate of return*; it is an interest rate that reflects the riskiness of the cash flows.

For example, we can value a two-year bond that is expected to pay a coupon of $80.00 in the first year, and a coupon of $80 plus the principal of $1,000 in two years when it matures (total payment in year 2 is $80 + $1,000 = $1,080). Let's assume that the appropriate interest rate or required rate of return is 6%. The first cash flow of $80.00 is equivalent to a present value of:

$$PV_1 = \$80.00/[1+6\%] = \$75.47$$

Next we need to bring the cash flow in year 2 of $1,080 back to today; we would do this by dividing by [1+ interest rate] twice. If we bring it back one year, the value of the $1,080 will be:

$$= \$1,080/[1+6\%] = \$1,018.87$$

If we bring this value back by one more year to today it will be worth:

$$PV_2 = \$1,018.87/[1+6\%] = \$961.20$$

There is also a formula which would have allowed us to bring this cash flow back in one step which involves dividing by [1+interest rate] twice; this formula is $PV_2 = \$1,080/[1+6\%]^2 = \$961.20$.

Therefore, today's value of a bond that pays $80 in the first year and $1,080 in the second year, is the sum of the present values of these two cash flows:

$$PV_1 + PV_2 = \$75.47 + \$961.20 = \$1,036.67$$

**We could theoretically use the above approach to value any investment where we know or can calculate what the expected cash flows are, and what the appropriate interest rate or required rate of return should be.**

The appropriate required rate of return is an interest rate that compensates the investor for the level of risk. We can think of it as being made up of two parts, the *risk-free* interest rate, which is the interest rate that we should be able to get for that period of time without taking any risk, plus a *risk premium* which compensates the investor for the additional risk of not getting their money back.

Government debt in developed countries is considered risk-free and it is this debt that defines what the risk-free interest rate is. There is an appropriate risk free rate for every period in time – for one year, for two years, for three years, for ten years and even for twenty years. These risk-free rates are established by the yields on risk-free government bonds for those maturities. If the two-year government bond has a yield of 2.5% - then the appropriate risk-free rate for two years would be 2.5%.

For bonds that are issued by stable companies, there is still some risk that the company will not be able to pay the coupon or repay the principal. Accordingly these bonds have to offer a slightly higher return than the risk-free bonds, and they will have a small risk premium. The required rate of return would be the risk-free rate plus the small risk premium, and the risk-free rate would still be a large part of the required rate of return. For risky issuers the risk premium is higher.

When the required rate of return rises, the term [1+ required rate of return] rises, and future cash flows become smaller when we discount them back to today by dividing by this larger number. **This means that if either the risk-free rate or the risk premium rises, the required rate of return will rise, and the value of the bonds will fall. In other words, if interest rates for a certain period rise (the risk-free rate rises), the price of a bond will fall. If a bond is seen to be more risky, its price will also fall. In both cases, the required rate of return has gone up.**

**The more the cash flows occur in the future, the more often they are discounted, and the more they are affected by a higher required rate of return.** The future cash flows are divided by a larger number [1 + required rate of return] more often. Therefore, longer-term bonds (and bonds with low coupons) are more affected by interest rate changes because their payments occur on balance more in the future. A bond with a shorter maturity (and a higher coupon) will pay out a larger proportion of its return earlier and would therefore be less affected by changes in the required rate of return.

Calculating the value of individual bonds is not something that we as investors would typically spend a lot of time doing; most bonds are trading at a fair price anyway. Buying bonds or having exposure to the bond market is however a great idea for most investors, and knowing the concepts behind valuing bonds allows us to think about what affects the bond market and what the drivers of value are for bonds – for example the importance of interest rates and the risk premium. Furthermore, these are topics that are spoken about in the investment world all day long.

A very common way for us to invest in fixed income investments is via funds, for example bond funds. A fund pools the money of many savers, and a professional will make the investment decisions as per the guidelines of the fund. We could for example invest in a US government bond fund, a UK gilt fund, or a large company corporate bond fund. In each case we would effectively be lending money to these borrowers via the funds. Investing via funds allows us to get an investment that is diversified and that gives us broad exposure to that asset class. We will discuss funds in more detail shortly.

**KEY QUESTIONS THAT WE CAN ANSWER AFTER READING THIS SECTION (CHECK THAT YOU CAN):**

1. WHAT IS A BOND?
2. WHO ARE THE MAIN ISSUERS OF FIXED INCOME/DEBT INVESTMENTS?
3. IF THE MATURITY IS LONGER, IS THE RETURN USUALLY HIGHER?
4. IS THE RETURN OF A BOND ALSO KNOWN AS ITS YIELD?
5. WHY ARE LONG-TERM INTEREST RATES TYPICALLY HIGHER THAN SHORT-TERM INTEREST RATES?
6. HOW CAN WE THEORETICALLY VALUE A BOND?
7. WHAT IS THE REQUIRED RATE OF RETURN? WHAT ARE ITS TWO PARTS?
8. WHAT IS THE RISK-FREE RATE?
9. WHAT IS THE RISK PREMIUM?
10. IS THERE A RISK-FREE RATE FOR DIFFERENT MATURITIES?
11. WHAT HAPPENS TO THE VALUE OF BONDS WHEN INTEREST RATES FOR THAT PERIOD RISE?
12. ARE CASH FLOWS THAT OCCUR FURTHER IN THE FUTURE MORE AFFECTED BY HIGHER INTEREST RATES?

**(THE ANSWERS CAN BE EASILY FOUND IN THIS SECTION)**

## 2.    EQUITY/STOCKS

**Investing in equity is the other main way that we as providers of capital or savers can make our money available to users of capital and compound returns. Investing in equity has historically offered some of the best returns for investors, but it also comes with some of the highest risks, since equity returns depend on how well companies do.**

**Although it is less common, investors can compound returns by investing in the private equity of private companies.** Private companies often do require outside capital for growth and will often take in private equity investors who provide capital in return for a part ownership of a company. In the early 1990s many new companies were created especially in the technology field, and private equity investing grew strongly. The stock market performed well in the late 1990s, and the original investors could exit their investments by selling stocks of these companies to the market via initial public offerings (IPOs) once the companies had reached a sufficient size. Taking the companies public is often the preferred end result for private equity investors - it means that the company is now large enough to be listed on a stock exchange and, accordingly that the valuation is higher.

**Private equity is usually held by the founders of the company and perhaps by a few outside equity investors as well.** This equity is not advertised in the newspaper and is not talked about as much since its performance is relevant for less people. **Private equity is also:**

*   *Illiquid* - it cannot be bought and sold easily without the price moving. Each transaction and investment is different and is usually negotiated on an individual basis;
*   *Riskier than the equity of larger companies* - the companies are typically early-stage companies and their products and services are less proven;
*   *Potentially able to offer a higher expected return* in order to make up for the greater risk. Another way of saying this is that because the company is smaller, an investor can buy a larger percentage of the equity for less money.

**Given the characteristics of private equity, the investors that invest in private equity are often sophisticated companies that specialise in private equity investing.** For most of us, it would make sense to make private equity investments via a private equity fund where a professional investor manages the investments on our behalf. **Furthermore, given the higher risk and lower liquidity of private equity investments, we would typically invest in private equity once we had accumulated some level of savings and had some experience as investors.** In fact, in many countries, there are requirements for investors in private equity funds to have a certain minimum wealth and/or income.

**The more common way of accumulating returns as equity investors is by investing in the equity or the stocks and shares of large companies that are listed on the stock market.** Millions of investors are part owners of the many companies that have listed their equity on stock exchanges. McDonald's, the restaurant chain, has its shares listed on the New York stock exchange, and many investors are part owners of this company. Investors can also invest in The Walt Disney Corporation, which is responsible for Mickey Mouse, Walt Disney World®, Disneyland®, a lot of movies, and other entertainment related products – these shares are also listed on the New York Stock Exchange. We can invest in BP, one of the largest oil companies in the world, whose shares are listed primarily on the London Stock Exchange. We can invest and be part owners of the company that sells Coca-Cola, Sprite and other beverages, by buying the shares of the Coca-Cola Company that trade on the New York Stock exchange. We can invest in the company that makes Mercedes Benz cars, Jeeps and Chrysler minivans by buying the shares of Daimler Chrysler, which are traded on the New York Stock Exchange and the Frankfurt Stock Exchange.

Equity investors that own small stakes in companies by owning the companies' shares/stocks include individual investors, big professional investors that manage large sums of money on behalf of many smaller investors, and insurance companies that collect insurance premiums that they have to manage until claims come in and a part of their funds has to be paid out. An equity investor benefits from the performance of a company based on the number of shares owned; an investor that owns 10 stocks of a company that has one million shares outstanding owns 0.001% (10/1,000,000 x 100%) of the company and this stake would move up and down with the overall value of the company's equity accordingly.

**A company's shares will typically trade on a stock exchange in the country in which it is based** - the stocks of leading American companies trade during market hours on stock exchanges in the United States - the New York Stock Exchange (NYSE), NASDAQ and others. Leading British companies trade on the London Stock Exchange. Leading companies in Japan trade on the Tokyo Stock Exchange; leading French companies trade on the Paris Stock Exchange and so on. Apart from the main exchanges for very large companies, most countries have other exchanges for slightly smaller companies as well. Which exchange a company lists its shares on has to do with where the company is based, how long it has been operating for, whether or not it is profitable, how long it has been profitable for, and how large it is.

A company that is listed in its home market, and that is trying to attract investors from another country, can also list its shares in that second country via what is known as a dual listing. The shares of Nokia, the Finnish mobile handset manufacturer, trade not only in Helsinki, Finland, but also on the New York Stock Exchange, because this allows the company to have easier access to the large number of investors that invest in technology stocks in the US.

Aside from being places where the stocks of a certain country trade, some stock exchanges market themselves as places where certain types of companies trade. The NASDAQ exchange, for example, markets itself as a stock exchange for companies 'seeking to transform the way that we live' – many growth companies especially technology companies trade on NASDAQ.

Many stock exchanges have physical locations, where providers of capital or their representatives or brokers, and users of capital, meet and exchange shares. Other stock exchanges allow buyers and sellers to transact via computers or the telephone. Over time, more and more physical exchanges have been replaced by computer-based systems, which allow more efficient trading.

**Information about stock prices and stock markets is provided in most newspapers, particularly in national newspapers and the newspapers of the larger cities where the stock exchanges are located.** The following is what a typical page from the financial section of one of these newspapers might look like:

| Stock | Price | Chng | 52 week | | Yld | P/E | Vol |
|---|---|---|---|---|---|---|---|
| | | | High | Low | | | 1000s |
| 3M | 124.04 | +1.41 | 131.60 | 86.00 | 2.0 | 29.0 | 9275 |
| AbbtL | 38.00 | +.50 | 57.98 | 29.80 | 2.5 | 13.7 | 23230 |
| Abrc&Ftch | 24.00 | +1.01 | 33.85 | 16.21 | 0 | 12.4 | 6986 |
| ABM Ind | 16.84 | -0.88 | 19.75 | 12.48 | 2.1 | 24.1 | 562 |

The list would then continue in alphabetical order. This table shows:

- *Name of the Stock/Company:* which is sometimes abbreviated to save space. 3M is an industrial company that makes tape and post-it notes among other things; AbbtL is Abbott Labs - a pharmaceutical company; Abrc&Ftch is Abercrombie & Fitch (a clothing company) and so forth;
- *Price:* the most recent price of the stock in the local currency. If the newspaper came out in the morning, this would often be the previous day's closing price;
- *Chng:* the change in the price on the day at the time of printing from the previous day;
- *52 week High/Low:* the highest and lowest prices at which the stock has traded during the last 52 weeks;
- *Yld (Dividend Yield):* the recent 12 month dividend divided by the stock price;
- *P/E Ratio:* the price/earnings ratio for the stock;
- *Vol 1000s (Volume 1000s):* the number of shares that have traded.

Sometimes the following are also included:

- *Close:* the closing price - the last price of the stock for that day's trading;
- *Open:* the opening price - the first price of the stock on that day's trading;
- *High:* the highest price of the stock for that particular day;
- *Low:* the lowest price of the stock for that particular day;

The newspaper that provides this market data will usually give the definitions for the terms used in their tables.

**Looking at stocks in the financial pages of a newspaper is quite a detailed way of looking at specific stocks and companies. When investors or the press speak about stocks more generally, they often use certain descriptive terms to categorise them – some of the most common terms include:**

- *Blue Chip Stocks:* stocks of large and well-known established companies, which usually have a large number of employees, multiple business activities in numerous countries, and are often considered to have strong management. Blue chip stocks are expected to be more stable because the companies are not dependent on any one product or region;
- *Growth Stocks:* stocks that are experiencing growth in revenues and earnings because they operate in industries that are growing strongly, in large part irrespective of how the general economy is doing. Growth stocks are often associated with new technologies;
- *Cyclical Stocks:* stocks whose revenues and earnings are strongly affected by the economy and less by the inherent growth of the business that they are in. The performance of car and steel stocks, for example, depends heavily on the economy;
- *Defensive Stocks:* stocks that are resilient in a downturn in either the stock market or the economy because demand for their products is relatively unaffected by the business cycle. They are considered to be safer than most other stocks, because they are usually not as highly valued and usually not as dependent on specific technologies or products for their success.

A company that is a growth stock today, could be a defensive stock in a few years as the area that they operate in becomes more mature. Alternatively a stock that is considered defensive today might not be in a few years if their business becomes more risky.

**Besides following the equity of companies by looking at individual share prices, we can follow an entire stock market or portion of the stock market by following a stock market index.** Stock market indices such as the S&P 500 take a number of stocks, for example all of the stocks that meet certain criteria, and look at them as a group. By following the numerical value of the index, we can follow the performance of an entire market or a segment of a market. The value of an index is calculated using one of a limited number of different methods.

**The value of a *market-capitalisation weighted* index is calculated by adding up the market capitalisations (the market values of the equity – the share price multiplied by the number of shares) of all of the companies in that index and dividing this number by an arbitrarily selected fixed number to get the number down to an easily followed number like 1,000.** For example, if the sum of all the market capitalisations in an index is 23,450,540,340,000 – this number could be divided by 23,450,540,340 to give us 1,000; this number would then act as the starting point for the index. The current level for the index would be all of the market capitalisations added up and again divided by 23,450,540,340. The weight of any company in the index would be calculated by dividing that company's market capitalisation, by the market capitalisation of all of the companies in the index. These calculations would be done on a continuous basis by computers.

**The value of a *price-weighted index* is calculated by adding up the share prices of the companies in the index and again dividing by a fixed number to get a number that can be easily followed such as 1,000 or 100.** The weight of any particular company in the index would be that company's share price divided by the sum of all of the share prices in the index. Using the share price alone to calculate index values is less common because the price of a stock is not a good indicator of a company's equity value; the price of a stock multiplied by the number of shares, known as the market capitalisation, is what the market value of the equity is.

Most indices were initiated many years ago and it was at that time that the level was set at an easily recognisable number such as 1,000 or 100. The most followed indices are:

- *The S&P 500:* a market-capitalisation weighted index of the 500 most widely owned companies in the United States. The index had a base level of 10 in 1941-43;
- *The NASDAQ Composite Index:* a market-capitalisation weighted index of all of the companies (US and International) that trade on the NASDAQ. The index was started at an arbitrary initial level of 100 on February 5, 1971;
- *The Dow Jones Industrial Average:* a price-weighted index of 30 blue chip companies in the US that are considered to be the leaders in their respective industries;

- *The FTSE 100 Index:* a market-capitalisation weighted index of the top 100 UK companies;
- *The DAX:* a market-capitalisation weighted index of thirty German blue chip companies traded in Frankfurt. The base value was 1,000 on Dec. 31, 1987;
- *The CAC 40:* a market-capitalisation weighted index of the forty most important companies listed in France on the Paris Bourse. The index had a base level of 1,000 on December 31, 1987;
- *The Nikkei 225 Index:* a price-weighted index of 225 companies listed on the Tokyo Stock Exchange. The index was started on May 16, 1949;
- *Topix (Tokyo Price Index):* a market-capitalisation weighted index of all companies listed on first section (for the largest companies) of the Tokyo Stock Exchange;
- *The Hang Seng:* a market-capitalisation weighted index of the 33 most important companies listed on the stock exchange of Hong Kong. The index had a base level of 100 on July 31, 1964.

Not all indices refer to a particular stock market, some are for certain sectors of the economy such as the *SOX,* the *Philadelphia Semiconductor Index,* which is a price-weighted index of stocks of companies that are involved in the design, manufacture and distribution of semiconductors. (This index had a base value of 100 on December 1, 1993).

A shareholder's return is the difference between where shares are bought and where they are sold, plus any dividends received. For example, if we bought one stock for $20 and sold it for $25 and we received a $1 dividend, then our return would effectively be $6 for an investment of $20, or 30% in percentage terms. The portion of this return that is made up by the dividend is ($1/$20 x 100%) or 5% - the *dividend yield* for this stock is 5%. Stock market indices also have a dividend yield, which is defined by the dividends that the stocks in the index pay over a year. The total annual return of a stock market index is the capital appreciation of the index (the numerical price move) plus the dividend yield for the index.

The dividend yield represents a very real return to shareholders, and most companies pay out a portion of their net income as dividends to provide a return to shareholders while they own the shares. Without the dividend, a shareholder would not have a cash return until he sold the shares – until then, the price return would only exist on paper. A company that does not need to reinvest in its business, perhaps because it is in a mature business area, will typically pay out a greater percentage of it net income in the form of dividends. A company that wants to reinvest aggressively in its business, will typically pay out a lower dividend and instead *retain* the earnings. As a shareholder, theoretically we would like the company to pay out a dividend if we can do more with the cash than the company can; and we would like the company to retain the earnings if the company can do more with the cash by reinvesting it than we can.

**As a shareholder in a large public company, we are one of the many shareholders or owners who have entrusted their money to the management of the company.** We often never see the company ourselves, nor can we supervise the management directly. We are relying to a large extent on the management to make decisions that create value and deliver a return to us; we therefore need to have confidence that the management keeps our interests in mind and works to improve the value of the equity. Fortunately, there are reasons why managements and companies should act in the best interest of shareholders:

- *Managers and employees often own stock* and therefore their interests are aligned with those of other shareholders - both benefit from share price rises. Also, the management is often compensated based on share price performance in the form of additional cash or additional shares;
- *The amount of money that companies can borrow and the cost of debt* are determined by the market value of the equity among other factors. Having a high value for the equity ensures that leverage is at a reasonable level and that the cost of debt is reduced;
- The company might want to *come back to the market and sell shares again.* In this case, a high share price is more desirable. The higher the share price, the more money the company can receive for a certain percentage of the company. If the owners come to the market to sell shares, they will get more money for the shares that they sell as well;
- *Upward share price movements create positive publicity* – if a company's shares are performing well, the company is seen to be successful, which in turn can affect business positively. A company that is losing a lot of value is likely to cause customers to wonder whether the company will be around in a few years;

- *The company might want to make an acquisition* by using its shares. If a publicly quoted company wishes to buy another company, the buying company will often use its own shares and offer them to the shareholders of the company that is being bought. With more highly valued shares, the company has to offer fewer shares in order to make the deal attractive to the shareholders of the company being bought. Also, a higher value of the buying company means that their shareholders control more of the company that is created once the two are merged.

Having a good share price performance is clearly very important for equity investors that want to get a return and compound their money. On the other hand, shareholders are very important for companies because they provide capital to companies, and as a group, determine the company's share price by buying and selling the shares. Fortunately, as we can see, having a strong share price is also very important for the companies - the users of capital, and that is why publicly quoted companies spend a great deal of time and money providing information about their business to the market, to ensure that the share price adequately reflects the noteworthy aspects of the company. Large companies have investor relations departments that focus on maintaining a constructive dialogue with investors, financial analysts and the press.

**Despite what overall seems like a fairly elegant way for users and providers of capital to interact, some people believe that there is always a winner and a loser when it comes to investing in stocks.** Often they believe that no one wins except the experts and/or that only the brokers make money, by charging their commissions for buying and selling stocks. Financial markets today however play such an important role in our society, that the vast majority of market participants have a vested interest in seeing them work efficiently as places for mutually beneficial transactions to take place between providers and users of capital – in response to the criticisms, there are a number of important points that have to be kept in mind:

- *When buy or sell decisions are made, no one should have access to better information regarding how a stock will perform in the future.* When important new information does come out, stock market regulations in most developed markets require the news to be simultaneously released to the entire market via a web site announcement or an official press release. Using material information that has not been publicly disclosed is insider trading and is illegal in most countries. ***Decisions to buy or sell are therefore ultimately based on different views held by the buyer and the seller.*** One party might have been right in selling a share and the other wrong in buying it, but when the decisions were made, both parties had an equal theoretical shot at being right, and that is what is important. Usually, the party that has done more work to understand the company and its potential valuation will be the one that takes the right decision;

- ***Stocks are often sold for reasons that do not relate to the fundamentals of the company or its valuation. The decision is based on a different preference.*** For example a stock might be sold because of a preference for cash. Both the buyer and the seller can end up happy because the seller gets the money, and the buyer gets the stock;

- A short-term investor might sell a stock after it has gone up 5% in the short term, and a longer-term investor might buy it with the view that over the next five years, the stock will go up even more. ***Different investors have different time horizons.***

Of these three reasons, the first is the most important – stocks are most often traded because the buyer and seller have different views regarding the company. It is important to remember that **no one can ever be certain about how a company will perform and what a company's share price will do, especially in the short-term, because no one will ever have perfect information regarding the future of a company.** How a company ultimately performs will be affected by many factors including:

- ***Competition:*** Is the competition increasing? Are the competitors offering better products or services?

- ***Price Developments:*** Are selling prices increasing? Is there a threat from cheaper substitutes?

- ***Costs:*** Are the costs of employees going up or down? Is the cost of the company's raw materials going up? Is the amount of money that the company makes on each product less?

- ***Management:*** Is management focusing on the right businesses? Are managers thrifty with their investments or are they spending money on unnecessary items like inappropriately lavish offices or unnecessary luxury items? Is management able to attract the right people and create the right structure for the company to be successful? Is management leaving the company and/or selling their shares?

- *Growth rate of the company:* How many more products is the company selling this year compared to last year? Is the overall market for the products growing and, if so, for how much longer can it grow? Are revenues growing or declining?

**In addition to all of the ways that these factors can develop, things can happen that no one expects** - a factory can be shut because of a fire, a business unit can be disrupted because of the illness of a manager, a company can be sued for defective products. Because of the uncertainty associated with how companies can develop and how share prices can move, investing in stocks always comes with a lot of uncertainty. Good investors invest based on an understanding of the industry and the company, and assess what is most likely to happen in the longer term, and they diversify their investments by holding a number of investments – more on this later. Based on their assessment of a company, they determine what they think the value of the company should be.

For the restaurant in our earlier example in Chapter II, the value of the equity increased exactly by the amount of net income that was not paid out as dividends. When a company trades in the stock market, the *book value*, which is the value shown on the balance sheet, will still increase by the amount of the net income that is not paid out in dividends, but the market price of the equity which is determined by the many investors that participate in the stock market, can be quite different from the book value. **Investors will value the company not only based on its book value, but also based on its ability to generate cash flows for the equity investor in the future - in the same way that investors value bonds based on the future cash flows that they provide.** Furthermore, the company might have 'assets' like a brand name or a proprietary ways of doing business that are not captured on the balance sheet; the market price of the equity will also take the value of these *intangible* assets into account.

**Valuing equity by valuing the cash flows that go to equityholders is more challenging than it is for most bonds. First of all, the cash flows theoretically last forever or until the company no longer exists. Secondly the cash flows depend on how the company does as per the income statement, and are therefore more difficult to calculate. And lastly this is true because the required rate of return is more difficult to calculate and it has a major impact on the calculated value.** (The required rate of return for the stock will be higher than that used for the debt of the same company because we know that equity is riskier than debt - bondholders are always entitled to their cash flow first). In contrast to equity, when we use the method of discounting cash flows for a bond, we are given the cash flows (coupons), they take place for a limited amount of time (to maturity) and the required return for most bonds depends a lot of the risk-free rate, which we can easily get from the yield of a government bond of the same maturity.

**To figure out the cash flows that go to equityholders we would need to build models of the financial statements of the company going forward to see how revenues, costs and net income might develop and therefore what the cash flows for the equity might be.** We have already learned about two of the three financial statements - the balance sheet and the income statement. The last financial statement that investors use is the cash flow statement, which summarises the actual cash flows that affect the company. The cash flow statement is usually divided into three sections to categorise where the cash flows take place – in operations, investing or financing. An example of a cash flow statement is shown below:

| | |
|---|---|
| **Operations** | |
| Net Income | 25,000 |
| Depreciation | 4,000 |
| Decrease in Inventories | 500 |
| Cash Flow from Operations | 29,500 |
| | |
| **Investing** | |
| Van bought | -20,000 |
| | |
| Cash Flow from Investing | -20,000 |
| | |
| **Financing** | |
| Bank loan | 10,000 |
| Proceeds: Outside Investor | 10,000 |
| Cash Flow from Financing | 20,000 |
| **CHANGE IN CASH** | **$29,500** |

**The financial statements of a company: the income statement, the balance sheet and the cash flow statement can be found in the company's Annual Report or on its website.** The annual report, published each year, describes a company's state of business and financial situation. An independent auditor checks the report for accuracy. If we wanted to learn about a company, we could learn a lot by looking at the company's annual report and the financial statements.

**To value the equity, we would need to predict the cash flows that go to equityholders, using the cash flow statement with some slight modifications, and we would need to discount them back to today using a required rate of return.** The required return would again be calculated using a risk-free rate and a risk-premium, in this case a risk premium to compensate us for the risk of investing in the stock. The risk free rate would be taken from a very long-term government bond because the expected cash flows in the case of equity should extend far into the future. The risk premium for the stock is related to how much the returns of that stock vary year to year compared with the overall market, and how much extra return the stock market should deliver over the risk-free rate to compensate investors for taking the extra risk. Predicting the cash flows that go far into the future requires a lot of assumptions and there is a lot of uncertainty in calculating the required rate of return; these numbers have a big impact on the calculated value as we shall see.

The challenges of valuing stocks can be illustrated by looking at an example of four hypothetical stocks and their cash flows:

| YEAR | CASH FLOWS | | | |
|---|---|---|---|---|
| | STOCK A | STOCK B | STOCK C | STOCK D |
| 1 | 1 | 1 | 0.2 | 0.2 |
| 2 | 1.1 | 1.1 | 0.4 | 0.4 |
| 3 | 1.2 | 1.2 | 0.8 | 0.8 |
| 4 | 1.3 | 1.3 | 1.6 | 1.6 |
| 5 | 1.4 | 1.4 | 3.2 | 3.2 |
| Growth After Yr 5 | 8% | 9% | 6% | 9% |

Let's assume that these cash flows have been predicted based on financial statements, industry information and other sources for the first five years. After five years, analysts often assume that there are too many unknowns to build detailed financial models for every year, so they assume a growth rate for the cash flows into the future. To arrive at the value for each of these stocks, these cash flows need to be discounted back to today. Let's assume that the correct required rate of return is 10%. We won't go into the details of the calculations, but when we calculate the values of the stocks, we come up with the following:

| | STOCK A | STOCK B | STOCK C | STOCK D |
|---|---|---|---|---|
| STOCK VALUE | $51.42 | $99.23 | $56.85 | $220.77 |

**We can see that stock B is valued almost twice as highly as stock A, even though it has identical cash flows per share for the first five years, and the growth rate differs by only 1% after that.** Stocks C and D have a very high growth rate for the first five years and then the growth rate flattens out – in one case at 6%, in the other at 9% - again the impact of the different growth rates on valuation is tremendous – stock D is valued at four times the value of stock C.

**The required rate of return also has a huge impact on the value calculated.** As the required rate of return goes up, the value of the stock falls significantly as the large number of cash flows that extend into the future are divided by a higher number to bring them back to present values.

| REQUIRED RETURN | STOCK A | STOCK B | STOCK C | STOCK D |
|---|---|---|---|---|
| 10% | $51.42 | $99.23 | $56.85 | $220.77 |
| 11% | $34.27 | $49.64 | $44.30 | $107.54 |
| 12% | $25.69 | $33.11 | $35.98 | $69.87 |
| 13% | $20.55 | $24.84 | $30.06 | $51.09 |

If a required return of 12% is used instead of a required return of 10%, the calculated value for Stock A is about half of what it was when the 10% rate was used, and Stock B is worth about one third of what it was.

Clearly valuing stocks is not that easy. A large part of valuing stocks involves imagining what the world or particular areas of the economy and companies might look like in five or ten years, and then trying to model this using financial statements. If we expect a company to grow significantly in the future, then by buying a stock in this company we would benefit if this company does grow and its equity value increases. The price that we can buy it at is important since it might already reflect this positive outcome; and as we can see, calculating the price is not that easy. There are many professionals that do this all day long, and even they have difficulty getting it right as we shall see in the next section. Stock markets as a whole (and bond markets) have however offered very significant returns for investors over time, so saving using these investments is nonetheless incredibly important. We will see how to get a broader exposure to equities (and bonds) in the next section.

**Theoretically, if all of the data were perfect, discounting future cash flows would be the best valuation method, but because of the assumptions and the effort required to value equity in this way, other valuation methods are often used to compare and analyze equity investments.** Typically, these valuation methods are much easier to calculate - they only look only at one or two numbers. Let's look at these valuation methods briefly:

- *P/E Ratio – (the Price-to-Earnings Ratio):* this is probably the most widely known valuation measure. It divides the share price by the earnings per share or EPS. The EPS are the net income or profits *per share* (Net Income ÷ Number of Shares). The earnings used are either this year's earnings, next year's earnings or in some cases last year's earnings. The P/E ratio gives the same result as taking the market capitalisation (share price x the number of shares) and dividing by the net income. The ratio gives the cost of each dollar of earnings, therefore a low P/E Ratio is a good thing, all other things being equal. One of the drawbacks of the P/E ratio is that it only looks at one year of earnings, and that the earnings of this one year are affected by depreciation, extraordinary charges and the growth rate of earnings, which might mean that a stock that looks expensive in one year might no longer look that way when looking at another year, or vice versa;

- *Price/Sales or Price/Revenues multiple:* many early-stage companies do not have earnings; sometimes earnings are distorted for a period of time because of extraordinary non-recurring expenses. The Price-to-Sales measure is a quick and easy-to-use valuation measure, along the lines of the P/E ratio, where companies are compared on the basis of sales; because shareholders care about earnings and other cash flows more than sales, comparing stocks on this basis indirectly assumes that sales would translate into similar earnings if normal earnings were there. Again we are only using one year's worth of data to determine the valuation with the drawbacks noted above;

- **_Enterprise Value (EV) to EBITDA Ratio:_** EBITDA (Earnings Before Interest, Taxes, Depreciation and Amortisation) is a measure of the operating earnings of a company, which go to both equity and debtholders. (Amortisation is a non-cash charge similar to depreciation). The EV to EBITDA measure divides the _Enterprise Value_ (the sum of the market value of the company's equity and net debt (debt minus cash)) by the total operating earnings of the company; we can see how conceptually it is similar to the P/E ratio except that it looks at more of the company, and the cash flows that go to more of the company;

- **_Price to Book Ratio:_** this measure takes the market value of a company's equity and divides it by the book value of the company's equity as it would appear on the balance sheet. As we said, a company will trade at an equity valuation that is determined by investors, a valuation that also reflects future cash flows and intangible assets. The book value of the equity is the accounting book value of the assets minus the debt on the balance sheet. By dividing the price of the equity by its book value, we the can see the premium that the market is assigning to the equity over its book value. Companies that have a lot of tangible assets, for example machinery companies, often trade at price to book values that are close to 1, companies that have a lot of intangible assets, like for example internet companies, can trade at book values much higher than 1;

- **_Dividend Yield:_** This measure looks at how much, in percentage terms, would be returned to the shareholder in the form of the earnings that are paid out as dividends. It divides the dividend by the share price, recognising that the dividend is a very real form of return that shareholders receive.

The value of a company and the conclusions that are drawn about whether investing in a stock is a good idea, in theory should not vary according to the valuation method used, but there can be practical difficulties with some valuation measures - in terms of either getting the data or in terms of being able to make the assumptions. The choice of valuation method used depends on the information available and often industry convention as well. Stock analysts frequently look at and compare stocks based on a number of different measures.

**Performing the calculations, making the necessary assumptions, and selecting the appropriate valuation method, combined with the fact that we never know exactly what will happen with the company in the future,**

makes the process of stock selection challenging. Before we invest in any individual stock we should look at its valuation and assess whether it appears cheap based on what we think is likely to happen with the company. Whenever we invest in equities, we need to appreciate that there is always risk and uncertainty involved, and that the assumptions can have a huge impact on the calculated value.

Equity and stocks as a group in many markets have risen over long periods of time and this is certainly something that we can make use of if we expect this to continue based on the interaction that we as providers of capital can have with companies. How we can do this is what we are going to look at next.

KEY QUESTIONS THAT WE CAN ANSWER AFTER READING THIS SECTION (CHECK THAT YOU CAN):

1. WHAT ARE THE CHARACTERISTICS OF PRIVATE EQUITY?
2. WHERE DO COMPANIES LIST THEIR SHARES?
3. IS EVERY SHAREHOLDER A PART OWNER OF THE COMPANY?
4. WHAT ARE STOCK MARKET INDICES AND HOW ARE THEY CALCULATED?
5. WHY IS HAVING A GOOD SHARE PRICE IMPORTANT FOR COMPANIES AND MANAGEMENTS?
6. CAN WE BE SURE ABOUT WHAT A STOCK WILL DO IN THE FUTURE AND WHY OR WHY NOT?
7. HOW CAN WE THINK ABOUT VALUING A STOCK OR EQUITY IN GENERAL?
8. WHAT ARE SOME OF THE DIFFICULTIES ASSOCIATED WITH VALUING STOCKS?
9. WHAT IS AN ANNUAL REPORT AND WHAT ARE THE THREE MOST COMMON FINANCIAL STATEMENTS?

(THE ANSWERS CAN BE EASILY FOUND IN THIS SECTION)

## 3.   MUTUAL FUNDS OR UNIT TRUSTS

**Instead of investing in individual debt investments or stocks directly, it is possible to get a broader exposure to equity and debt through funds, bearing in mind that although individual investments might be difficult to value, both the equity and debt markets have risen historically over time.** These funds are known as *mutual funds* in the United States and Canada, *unit trusts* in Great Britain and Australia and as *public funds* in some countries such as Germany (public funds because everyone is allowed to invest in them). They are great investments for almost all savers – the key is to understand how they work and what to look out for.

**A mutual fund or unit trust is a pool of money that consists of the money of many individual investors like us that have contributed to the fund.** A professional investor, known as the *fund manager* or *portfolio manager*, then manages the money and makes the individual investments. The fund will have guidelines that dictate what the fund is supposed to invest in, and the fund manager is responsible for selecting the best investments for the fund, based on the guidelines. The guidelines might specify that the fund will invest in large US companies, or in large European companies, or in emerging market debt for example. Based on its guidelines, an appropriate benchmark or index is also selected, against which the performance of the fund and therefore the fund manager are measured.

**Investing via funds can provide numerous advantages over investing in individual stocks or bonds directly. Firstly, a professional fund manager is given the responsibility of selecting the investments**. This fund manager should be able to look at the investments in much greater detail than the average individual investor can – that is his/her job and what he or she focuses on all day long. The manager can also meet with the companies, build financial models to establish the value of securities, and make use of a research department that performs in-depth analysis on the investments. **Furthermore, a fund provides exposure to a lot of stocks or bonds at the same time and is therefore a diversified investment.** With $1,000 it would be difficult to buy all of the stocks in the S&P 500 index to capture the performance of that entire index (which contains 500 stocks), whereas we could put $1,000 into an S&P 500 Mutual Fund and capture a large part of the performance of the index. The fund would also reweight its investments based on the changing weights of the stocks in the index.

**The guidelines of the unit trust or mutual fund might allow the fund to invest in a certain country, in one sector of the stock market, or in a segment of the bond market.** There are thousands of mutual funds in existence, and there is an almost infinite number of funds that could be created – funds that invest only in the debt of North American governments, funds that invest only in the equity of environmentally friendly companies, funds that invest purely in the equity of automotive companies, or funds that invest only in companies that are based in Africa and so on. Some very common types of mutual funds are:

- *US Equity Funds* that invest exclusively in the equity of US companies – the benchmark could be the S&P 500 index;
- *UK Equity Funds* that invest exclusively in the equity of UK companies – the benchmark could be the FTSE 100 index;
- *Sector Funds* that invest in the best companies in particular sectors, for example the pharmaceutical or technology sectors perhaps on a global basis. The benchmark for a semiconductor fund could be the SOX index. During periods where certain sectors are performing well, these funds would be able to capture this performance;
- *Emerging Market Stock Funds* that invest in the equity of emerging market companies;
- *Government bond funds* that invest in the government bonds of a certain country.

**Mutual funds or unit trusts can be either actively or passively managed.** Actively managed funds over- or underweight investments relative to their benchmark in order to try to beat the performance of the index. The fund manager of an actively managed US equity fund with the S&P 500 as its benchmark, would try to perform better than the index by making active investment decisions. He or she would weight a stock in the fund differently from the weight of that stock in the benchmark if he or she had a view on how the stock will perform. If the fund manager thinks that a stock that has a weighting of 2% in the index will not do as well as the index - that it will underperform - he or she will invest less than 2% of the fund in that stock and invest more in other stocks that he or she thinks will do better. If he or she thinks that the stock will do better than the index - that it will outperform - then he or she will invest more than 2% in the stock and less in other stocks. If these views are wrong, and the fund manager bets on the wrong stocks, then he or she will underperform the benchmark.

**As opposed to being actively managed, funds can also be passively managed. Funds that are passively managed weight all of the securities as closely as possible to their weights in the benchmark or index.** In other words, the fund manager does not take any active bets. Changes to the holdings in the fund would be mechanical, as the weights of the stocks in the index change with prices changes, or other events such as share issues. **Passively managed funds are also known as *index funds*, because they aim to replicate the index as closely as possible.** Index funds also usually automatically reinvest the dividends back into the stocks that make up the index, which means that we do not have to do it, and that the money is always at work in the index. **Index funds have become popular because they are lower cost (the fund management process is cheaper) and because active management strategies have come under criticism - particularly for stock funds but also for bond funds in developed markets.**

The following are some of the main strategies that active portfolio managers use to try and beat a benchmark or index, and some of the criticisms that have come to light. These strategies are strategies that many of us would also try to use when selecting individual investments, so many of these issues are relevant for us as well.

**The first strategy that could be considered is market timing** - this strategy involves trying to time purchases when investments are thought to be at low prices, and selling them when they are thought to be at high prices. Makes sense, except that getting the timing right is very difficult in practice - one never knows when these moments of low or high prices are occurring ahead of time. Furthermore, recent performance tends to affect investor decisions. Investors often get more optimistic about an investment when it is performing well, and more negative about it when it is doing poorly. This can lead to putting more money into investments after their price has risen a lot, and selling after prices have fallen a lot - clearly not necessarily a good strategy for making money. This behavioural phenomenon is known as the *recency* effect. Trying to time the market can be costly, because history shows that if an investor misses particular periods during which the market performs very well, performance is severely affected.

**The second strategy that is often attempted is security selection** - this strategy involves over- and underweighting stocks or bonds based on what the investor thinks of the fundamentals of the investment. This would seem like a good strategy, except that many studies have shown that active managers have tremendous difficulty outperforming developed market indices using this strategy over any significant period of time. Picking the right investments in most markets has become too competitive because too many people are trying to do the same thing. If a stock or bond is cheap, some investors notice this almost immediately, and the price quickly adjusts based on the shares or bonds that are bought. The first few buyers out of the thousands trying to find mispricings might make a return, but all of the others will not. When the next mispricing occurs, because there are so many funds, it is unlikely that the same funds will again benefit by buying before the others. In other words no fund consistently outperforms, and since mistakes are bound to happen, the majority of actively managed funds in developed markets can not deliver a better performance than the index (or index funds) for the investor.

**The third and final strategy is sector selection.** The strategy involves over- and underweighting certain sectors of the market (for example the technology sector or the pharmaceutical sector) at certain times. This strategy typically does not work for the same reasons that stock selection usually does not work. Too many people are trying to do the same thing. Although different sectors do outperform over certain periods, one never knows ahead of time which ones and when with enough accuracy.

**When there were fewer mutual funds, and the funds were mainly competing against private individuals, fund professionals had a better chance of outperforming the market or index.** Private individuals are often less sophisticated in analysing the investments, and they often make investment decisions for personal reasons, such as a need for cash, as opposed to reasons that relate purely to the fundamentals of an investment. Today in most developed markets, like the United States, UK and European stock markets, mutual funds hold a large percentage of all of the available investments, so the market has become quite efficient. Furthermore, because the funds hold a large percentage of the investments, the average performance of mutual funds has to be very close to the performance of the market itself – they are the market.

**There are additional reasons that explain why most actively managed mutual funds underperform their benchmarks, as well as structural reasons that even highlight why it is difficult to evaluate mutual funds or unit trusts:**

- *Trading and management costs reduce performance.* Management costs, research costs and trading costs can easily be as high as 3% per year. The fund would have to outperform the benchmark by 3% just to match the benchmark;
- *The funds have to report their performance periodically* because investors want to see it. Decisions that lead to showing a good short-term performance are often inconsistent with showing a good long-term performance; the portfolio manager might have to chase a stock that is going up in the short-term, to show good monthly performance, instead of focusing purely on the long-term winners;
- *To evaluate an active portfolio manager against his benchmark, many years of data are needed.* By the time we have collected the data to ascertain whether the fund manager is doing well, a lot of time will have passed. We will have missed the performance, and who knows if the future performance will be as good. Any period of great performance has almost never been sustained over a meaningful period of time.

**To make the process of fund selection even more complicated, the largest single driver of fund performance is what the fund invests in - its benchmark.** The performance of actively managed funds is usually close to the benchmark (a little more, more often a little less) and passively managed funds perform almost identically to the benchmark. A Japanese equity fund will most likely outperform a US equity fund if Japanese equities outperform US equities. A technology fund will outperform a pharmaceuticals fund over a period during which technology stocks perform well. When the greatest driver of performance is the fund's benchmark (which is a decision that the fund manager does not take), then the key would be for us to select the funds with the benchmarks that will perform the best going forward. However, knowing which sector or benchmark will perform the best in the future is almost impossible to assess as well.

Another thing that can have a seriously bad effect on performance is switching between funds, which is typically done after a period of poor performance. Let's look at a stylised example of two funds and their performance over ten years:

**FUND A**

| YEAR 1 | YEAR 2 | YEAR 3 | YEAR 4 | YEAR 5 | YEAR 6 | YEAR 7 | YEAR 8 | YEAR 9 | YEAR 10 | |
|---|---|---|---|---|---|---|---|---|---|---|
| 5% | 6% | -2% | -3% | 7% | 9% | -6% | -2% | 9% | 10% | 36.29% |

**FUND B**

| YEAR 1 | YEAR 2 | YEAR 3 | YEAR 4 | YEAR 5 | YEAR 6 | YEAR 7 | YEAR 8 | YEAR 9 | YEAR 10 | |
|---|---|---|---|---|---|---|---|---|---|---|
| 5% | 6% | 3% | 6% | -4% | -3% | 10% | 2% | -2% | 9% | 35.62% |

Over the ten-year period, both funds provided a return of approximately 36%. If we assume that the investor looked at his fund and reassessed his investment options every two years, the behaviour of an investor that had put money into Fund A in Year 1 might have been:

- In Year 4, after two years of poor performance (-2%, -3%) he might have lost patience and sold Fund A to buy Fund B, which had shown very good performance in the previous two years (+3%, +6%);
- In Year 6, after two years of poor performance in Fund B (-4%, -3%), he might have sold Fund B and bought back Fund A which had shown two years of good performance (+7%, +9%);
- In Year 8, after two years of poor performance, (-6%, -2%), he might have sold Fund A for Fund B which had shown two years of very good performance (+10%, +2%).

The investor's performance over the ten years would have been:

**SWITCHING A/B-after underperformance**

| YEAR 1 | YEAR 2 | YEAR 3 | YEAR 4 | YEAR 5 | YEAR 6 | YEAR 7 | YEAR 8 | YEAR 9 | YEAR 10 | |
|---|---|---|---|---|---|---|---|---|---|---|
| 5% | 6% | -2% | -3% | -4% | -3% | -6% | -2% | -2% | 9% | -3.05% |

He would have received a return of –3%, versus the +36% that either of the two funds would have provided without switching. The performance would probably have been even lower because switching often costs money.

This example is extreme, in terms of the timing of the switches, and the difference in performance of the funds over certain periods, but it does illustrate the mental processes that can affect the performance of an investor. Does this mean that we should buy the fund that has underperformed the most? Not really because poor funds often just continue to underperform. **Historical performance, whether good or bad, does not say much about the future.**

Picking which funds to buy is very difficult even though some fund management companies have a better reputation than others – most studies indicate nonetheless that the vast majority of 'good' funds are statistically not going to beat their benchmark over the long term. Certain investors that have consistently shown excellent performance have become very famous (e.g. Warren Buffet, Peter Lynch, John Neff).

**This brings us back to index funds, which provide broad exposure to equity or debt by coming close to replicating the performance of a relevant index. They therefore outperform most actively managed funds in any one-year period and almost all of them over a longer period. They also cost less in terms of management fees and make following the fund performance easier – the fund will perform very much like the index. In light of these significant advantages, index funds are typically a preferred alternative for getting exposure to developed equity and bond markets, versus the vast majority of the more expensive actively managed funds.** Because it is can be very difficult to select which sector or market will do well ahead of time, a sensible investment approach might involve using some of our regular savings, and investing in a number of different index funds (to get a global bond and equity exposure); and allocating the same amount of money to each fund each month to make use of a technique known as dollar cost averaging. The considerations that are relevant for how much we should invest in bonds, how much equities, and how much in other investments, as well as some practical investment considerations are discussed in the next sections.

### KEY QUESTIONS THAT WE CAN ANSWER AFTER READING THIS SECTION (CHECK THAT YOU CAN):

1. WHAT IS A MUTUAL FUND OR UNIT TRUST?
2. WHAT ARE THE ADVANTAGES OF THESE FUNDS?
3. WHAT KINDS OF FUNDS ARE THERE?
4. WHAT HAS HISTORY SHOWN WITH RESPECT TO ACTIVE MANAGEMENT IN MATURE MARKETS?
5. WHY IS IT DIFFICULT FOR ACTIVELY MANAGED FUNDS TO BEAT THEIR BENCHMARK?
6. WHAT ARE THE MAIN ADVANTAGES OF INDEX FUNDS?

(THE ANSWERS CAN BE EASILY FOUND IN THIS SECTION)

## 4.   HEDGE FUNDS

**Hedge funds are often talked about in the press, and after a strong period of growth, hedge funds are today a major competitor to mutual funds and unit trusts for many investors. Hedge funds are often reserved for wealthy individuals and professional investors** who are thought to be better able to assess the risks and better able to afford a loss. Because good hedge funds are in demand, it can also be difficult for smaller investors, who effectively make less attractive clients, to access these funds. They can however be a very good addition to a portfolio once some assets have been saved up; furthermore, because they are spoken about so much, it is worth knowing what these products involve.

**Hedge funds are like mutual funds in that a professional invests a pool of money on behalf of the investors that have given money to the fund, but they differ from mutual funds in that:**

- *They tend to focus on absolute performance or capital preservation – just making money,* in contrast to mutual funds that move with the benchmark and are measured relative to a benchmark. Hedge funds are also often referred to as *absolute return funds*;
- *Hedge Funds often employ strategies that 'hedge' risks;* hedging a position involves taking a position that reduces or eliminates a certain risk. For example, a hedge fund based in the United States could invest in the UK stock market and hedge the currency risk of the British Pound going down versus the US Dollar. If a particular company has a car business is undervalued and a boat business that one does not want to invest in, a hedge fund could invest in the company, and hedge the boat industry exposure in order to benefit from the improvement in the car industry alone. It is possible to hedge many kinds of risk: currency risk, interest rate risk, etcetera;
- *Hedge funds are theoretically in a better position to make money whatever the market is doing,* because they do not have the benchmark that to a large extent dictates which investments the fund needs to own. Hedge funds can effectively try to make money based on mispricings across markets, across regions, or amongst almost any investments;

- *Hedge funds often employ leverage to increase returns when they feel confident about an investment.* Hedge funds will usually state in their description how much leverage they are looking to employ, so investors can get a sense of the risk from leverage. Leverage of course means that losses can also be greater when things go badly.

**The risks of investing in hedge funds can be more difficult to assess than the risks of investing in mutual funds or unit trusts.** Hedge fund risk is much more related to the quality of the hedge fund manager, whereas the biggest driver of mutual fund performance relates to what the benchmark will do – even most active mutual fund managers do not deviate that much from the benchmark since that would mean too much risk. To allow investors to assess the risk, hedge funds are increasingly required to disclose their strategies for making money. This might also limit the flexibility of hedge funds if they are bound to these disclosures. **To mitigate the risk of being invested in a particular hedge fund, numerous hedge funds are often bundled into a basket of hedge funds known as a fund of funds.**

**One of the things most commonly associated with hedge funds is short selling, which is often done in the context of hedging risks. Short selling allows a hedge fund to make money when an investment goes *down* in price. This is done by selling the investment without actually owning it.** For example, a hedge fund that does not own a stock could borrow it from someone else and sell it in the market. Once the price of the stock has gone down, the hedge fund could buy it back and return it to whomever it was borrowed from. The profit to the hedge fund would be the difference between the price at which it was sold at, and the price at which it was bought back at, minus any borrowing costs. For example, a hedge fund could borrow a stock that costs $40.00 from its original owner (via an intermediary like an investment bank) and sell it in the market. If the stock that was at $40.00 goes to $30.00, and the hedge fund buys it back at $30.00, the hedge fund has made $10.00, less a cost for borrowing the stock say $0.50. Their profit would be $9.50. After the stock has been bought back, the hedge fund would return it to the intermediary, and the intermediary would return it to the real owner. After the transaction the other fund ends up holding the stock as before and has earned $0.50 for lending it. Of course the short-seller can also be wrong. If the stock rises, the hedge fund could end up buying the stock back at a higher price; if they buy it back at $50.00, their loss is the sale price less the price where they bought it back, in this case a loss of $10.00, plus the borrowing cost – the total loss would be $10.00 + $0.50 = $10.50.

The reason that someone would lend their stock instead of selling it themselves, only to potentially see it drop in value if the short-seller is right, is either because they have a different view – they think it will go up, or because the stock is part of their index and they therefore almost have to hold some of it to avoid taking a big bet. Someone owns every stock, and the lender of the stock is at least guaranteed a return for lending it.

**Hedge funds have developed in order to take advantage of market opportunities that were not captured by traditional investors such as mutual funds.** If a majority of investors buy stocks because they think they are going up, the level of the stock market will probably reflect this expectation. There might be an opportunity for hedge funds to sell short some of the stocks whose prices exceed their true value. That is one way that hedge funds can make money. There are different types of hedge funds that employ different strategies to try to make money:

- ***Opportunistic hedge funds (including long/short equity and macro funds):*** long/short equity funds buy (or 'go long') stocks that they think will go up, and sell short (or 'go short') stocks that they think will go down. Many of these funds are market neutral in that they aim to generate a return that is not tied to movements in the overall market. Macro funds aim to generate returns by capitalising on macroeconomic factors such as interest rate differences, currency anomalies or inflation trends;

- ***Event-driven funds:*** these funds seek to benefit from differences in valuation of different securities surrounding an event like a merger, a spin-off or a restructuring. Merger arbitrage funds for example seek to benefit from the price difference between the stock of the company that is being bought, and that of the acquirer, when there is uncertainty whether the deal will go through. Distressed security funds buy the securities (often the bonds) of companies that are near bankruptcy, on the belief that the company will be able to avoid some of the financial difficulties that the market expects;

- ***Relative Value Funds:*** these funds try to profit from differences in valuation between different securities that provide a similar economic position. For example, a convertible bond can be replicated with a combination of bonds and stocks. A hedge fund could buy a convertible bond and sell short the appropriate combination of stocks and bonds to exploit a valuation difference between the two.

**Hedge funds are often blamed for increasing the volatility in the financial markets because they take large bets very quickly and because they are able to short-sell.** They probably do contribute to volatility, but if the price of an investment is being affected too much by a hedge fund, there is nothing stopping other investors from stepping in and buying if a hedge fund is selling aggressively, or selling it if a hedge fund is buying aggressively. This would reduce the price movement caused by the hedge fund. In a well-functioning securities market, investments ultimately find their true value sooner or later anyway - hedge funds are probably just a way for this to happen more quickly, where some investors are able to make money when the investment goes down as well as up.

Because they are less constrained in their investments, the first hedge funds in a certain area of the financial markets are often able to exploit mispricings. Good hedge fund managers are often sophisticated investors who are well positioned to find these mispricings.

**Hedge funds can be a very useful addition to an investment portfolio if we can get access to them.** The key is to believe in the manager and to feel comfortable with the strategy. Hedge funds are often able to do things that we could not do ourselves like short-selling, or operate in areas of the financial markets that we could not operate in in the same way – in this context hedge funds can be a very valuable addition to an investment portfolio once we have reached a certain level of sophistication and have some savings set aside.

KEY QUESTIONS THAT WE CAN ANSWER AFTER READING THIS SECTION (CHECK THAT YOU CAN):

1. WHAT IS A HEDGE FUND?
2. WHAT ARE THE DIFFERENCES BETWEEN HEDGE FUNDS AND MUTUAL FUNDS?
3. WHAT IS SHORT SELLING?
4. WHAT ARE SOME OF THE WAYS IN WHICH HEDGE FUNDS TRY TO MAKE MONEY?

(THE ANSWERS CAN BE EASILY FOUND IN THIS SECTION)

## 5.   REAL ESTATE

Real estate includes houses and apartments, and it also includes land, shopping malls and office buildings. There are two ways of investing in real estate: directly and indirectly. Direct real estate investing means owning, and having responsibility for managing the real estate, ourselves. Investing in real estate indirectly means investing via a company or a fund that makes the real estate investment decisions on our behalf.

### Direct Real Estate Investing

Real estate is different from other investments that we have spoken about, in that it is 'real'. We can stand on it, walk on it, and if a house or apartment has been built on it, even live in it. When we own a stock, we are part owners of a company, but often we never see the company or the share. Price trends in the real estate market also tend to persist for longer than those in the financial markets and misspricings probably last longer since less investors are typically looking at the same investments, and the investments are not as easy to buy and sell. Price swings can also be severe in a downturn or an upturn.

Buying and selling real estate can take a long time and a lot of effort, and the value of any piece of real estate is much more likely to be determined by what someone is willing to pay for it as opposed to pure financial measures. Transaction costs are also higher. Often there are also maintenance and refurbishment costs and administrative costs associated with owning real estate – things like painting walls, replacing light bulbs, fixing roofs, property taxes and insurance. For properties that are rented out, getting the financial return might also be more difficult, because collecting the money can be more difficult. When something goes wrong with a rental property there are often disputes about who is responsible for paying for what. This is in contrast to the stock market, which is a liquid and highly regulated market, where we probably never even see the stock physically, and where the obligations of the participants are usually very clearly defined.

**How real estate performs depends on a lot of factors, which can be thought of to a large extent as being supply and demand related including:**

- *The general economy:* if the economy is growing strongly and employment is rising, demand for housing should increase and so should prices. If wages fall or unemployment becomes a factor, then the opposite will probably happen;
- *Interest rates:* If the cost of borrowing falls, people will be able to afford larger mortgages (more leverage) and house prices often rise. If interest rates are rising or expected to rise, buyers often become more cautious and prices begin to fall. Leverage as always comes with risks;
- *Demographic/employment factors:* job creation and young people moving to an area is often good for house demand and prices. Separately, in many countries, the average age is rising, so areas that offer good weather and good recreational facilities for older people might see an increase in demand;
- *Transportation related factors:* A new train or a new roadway that provide a better connection for an area and that reduce commuting times can improve an area's desirability;
- *Supply:* a lack of supply of a particular type of real estate can cause prices to squeeze higher with increased demand. Conversely an increase in supply often reduces demand for other properties and has a dampening effect on prices.

**Different types of real estate are traditionally associated with different levels of risk.** The following is a list of the main categories of real estate:

- *Apartments (residential),* which are generally considered to be lowest risk, because they can be easily rented out and easily compared to similar units to get an idea of value;
- *Houses (residential)* like apartments can also usually be easily rented out. Because each one is more likely to be unique, and therefore less comparable, they bear a slightly higher risk;
- *Office Buildings and Hotels (commercial)* - demand for commercial real estate is more volatile and more linked to the economic cycle. Companies can quickly downsize or even move their operations to cut costs; hotel demand is also very linked to the economy and company budgets;
- *Undeveloped land (commercial or residential)* is considered highest risk; all properties are different and the farthest from completion. Planning regulations can play a role as well.

The above is a common-sense way of thinking about the risk of different types of real estate investments. As with any investment, the individual factors that can affect price should be looked at in detail. It could be, for example, that because of overbuilding of apartments, that the risk of investing in apartments at a point in time is higher than the risk of investing in other types of real estate.

**The most common real estate investment for most of us is the purchase of our home, and in many countries the government encourages home ownership, for example, by not taxing the appreciation or capital gain of our homes.** In some countries, the interest rate payments on a mortgage are also *tax deductible*, which means that we do not have to pay tax on the income that is used to make the mortgage payments. How the government specifically encourages home ownership can vary, by location, and also with time; the specific information can be gathered from government tax publications or on the Internet.

An investment in real estate, such as a home, with a mortgage, can be shown as below:

| HOUSE | DEBT/ MORTGAGE |
| | EQUITY |

**Although history shows that real estate prices have risen over long periods of time, house prices can and do also fall, and when they do, the effects of leverage will apply.** The percentage change in the equity will be greater than the percentage change in the value of the house. However, because our home is an asset that we often need and that costs a lot of money, borrowing money is often necessary to make the purchase. Additionally, mortgage interest rates are usually the lowest personal interest rates that we can get. If the value of our house falls in the short term, and we are living in the house and do not need to sell, it might also not matter that much, as long as we can make the interest rate payments.

**With all other real estate investments that are not our main residence, the effects of leverage will apply as well, and the appreciation that takes**

**place between purchase and sale is usually taxed, and so is any rental income.** This significantly reduces the return. In order for us to make money, the return has to be high enough to make up for this taxation and the other expenses associated with owning the property. Because most real estate assets are very expensive on a per unit basis compared to other investments, seeing the value of these assets drop can be disturbing especially when leverage is involved. Before making an investment of this type we need to think carefully about whether this is a good idea given the prospects for the object, the costs and the work involved, and the expenses and taxes that might reduce our return. Some investors have had the unfortunate experience of having the value of the asset drop so much that it is below the amount of debt that was used to buy it. This means that all of the equity is wiped out i.e. the ownership stake has gone to zero, and that they still owe money. When the asset is sold, they actually will not get back enough to even repay the debt. This is also known as *negative equity* and thinking about how the balance sheet would look when the asset on the left is smaller than the debt on the right, helps visualise why the equity is negative in order for the two sides to balance.

The two sources of return for a real estate investor are capital appreciation and rental income. Capital appreciation is the return that relates to the price of the property going up over time while it is owned by the investor. The rental income is the return generated from the rental receipts less the expenses. Whether the property is making money from the rental income can be summarised with a simple income statement like the one we looked at for a company in Chapter II, showing the rental income, annual expenses, taxes and ultimately a figure for the income. This clearly requires a bit of analysis regarding anticipated rental receipts (allowing for unrented gap periods), the expenses, as well as any taxes that have to be paid.

This subject clearly requires some analysis – but in principle, importantly, the rental return is significantly affected by the expenses related to managing the property and the interest expense. If a lot of debt is used to buy the asset (there is a lot of leverage), the rental return might be quite small. Clearly if the rental return is small, the return, if there is to be one, has to come from capital appreciation.

There is no doubt that real estate investing can make money for investors, but in order to assess whether it will make money, the factors that drive real estate prices have to be thought about, and the income statement should also be prepared using conservative assumptions - if too many people are trying to do the same thing without regards to valuation, this idea will usually not deliver a very good result.

**For professional real estate investors, investing in real estate is an active process – making money often involves more than just buying a property, renting it out or waiting, and selling it.** It often involves additional things like:

- *Renovating run-down properties* – where the buyer spends time and money to fix up a property to sell it a price that not only covers the investment made, but also allows for a return to be made;
- *Splitting a property into multiple units* – buying a larger property and creating multiple units that can then be separately rented out or sold;
- *Making use of government programs* that encourage investment in run-down neighbourhoods by offering cheaper financing and/or providing tax breaks to make the investment more attractive;
- *Financing techniques,* which allow the interest expense to be reduced. Sometimes sellers might lend money to the buyer at a lower rate than would otherwise be possible;
- *Understanding local regulations* that can have a big impact on how much money can be made on a property. If agricultural land can now be built on, the value of the land would rise significantly.

Becoming an active investor in real estate can be a great source of wealth; all kinds of deals, restructurings and renovations can be undertaken in order to create value; this however becomes a business in its own right, and goes beyond a normal savings and investing program.

Home ownership is something that makes sense for most people that are in one city for a longer period of time, and having some investments in real estate also makes a lot of sense from a diversification perspective. Additional real estate investments would have to be carefully examined. House prices can go up for long periods of time, but they do not go up forever and not in a straight line either. If everyone expects the price of houses to rise, then house prices will largely reflect this view - more people will be buying, people will be remortgaging to buy more, sellers would become more price sensitive. As a saver and investor, it is important to bear in mind the factors that will determine the future price of any real estate investment, and not to follow the herd blindly. Often real estate investors and investors in general make money by being early in discovering something that others have not yet realised or begun to appreciate.

## Indirect Real Estate Investing

**The other way to invest in real estate is indirectly - through a fund where a professional invests on behalf of a group of investors who have contributed money.** In the United States and Canada, one very common type of investment fund of this type is known as a *Real Estate Investment Trust* or *REIT.*

**Funds that invest in real estate typically invest in commercial real estate projects** – individual investments are larger, and there is more scope for the manager of the fund to add value. Because they invest in commercial real estate, which most people do not invest in directly, these funds can offer excellent diversification benefits. Additionally, this structure offers numerous other advantages:

- *Each investor is responsible for part of the overall investment so the minimum amount of money that one person has to commit to purchase real estate is much less.* In other words, what can be bought is much larger than any individual's investment;
- *A professional makes the investment decisions* and should be able to add value by doing a better job of selecting investments. Furthermore, many of the value creating actions that we described earlier, such as renovating the properties, can be undertaken more easily by a company;
- *There are economies of scale* - the cost of something per unit drops when the cost can be spread among multiple properties. For example, administrative and management fees can be shared between the properties;
- *The investment is more easily sold* because the funds often trade on a stock exchange.

The factors that drive the value of commercial real estate are very similar to the factors listed earlier for direct real estate investments, bearing in mind that commercial real estate tends to be more risky and volatile than residential real estate.

Indirect real estate investments can theoretically have characteristics that make them very interesting – because they provide a source of diversification, and because they allow us to benefit from professionals making investments in assets such as commercial real estate which we otherwise would probably not have access to. We would have to make sure that we feel comfortable with the manager of the assets, and that there is a financial argument that we can feel comfortable with as to why these assets should deliver a positive return. These funds are typically quoted on a stock exchange, so many of the valuation considerations that apply to stocks also apply to these investments. Because the stock market often rewards growth companies with higher valuations, than it does companies that generate a lot of cash (which these companies often do), we would need to look carefully at whether the investment can justifiably offer an attractive return. Each investment would need to be looked at on a case-by-case basis and should probably also be discussed with an investment professional. Indirect real estate investments are usually not the core element of a regular saving and investing plan, although they can play a role (stocks and bonds through funds often are).

KEY QUESTIONS THAT WE CAN ANSWER AFTER READING THIS SECTION (CHECK THAT YOU CAN):

1.  WHAT ARE SOME OF THE FACTORS THAT AFFECT REAL ESTATE RETURNS?
2.  HOW DOES THE GOVERNMENT ENCOURAGE HOME OWNERSHIP IN MANY COUNTRIES?
3.  WHAT IS INDIRECT REAL ESTATE INVESTING AND WHAT ADVANTAGES CAN IT PROVIDE?

(THE ANSWERS CAN BE EASILY FOUND IN THIS SECTION)

## 6. COMMODITIES

Commodities are physical substances or bulk goods which are interchangeable with each other if they are of the same type. A commodity is the opposite of a differentiated product. Commodities include energy products such as oil; metals such as gold, silver and aluminium; 'soft' commodities that cannot be stored for long periods of time such as agricultural products, sugar and orange juice; and livestock such as pork bellies. It is easier to invest in some commodities than in others – precious metals such as gold and silver can be purchased through most banks, whereas it is almost impossible for us to purchase pork bellies.

**When economic growth picks up, commodity prices often rise quite quickly** - while economic growth is slow, returns are often low, and there is very little investment to produce more of these products. When growth picks up, it takes some time to make more of these products available, in the meantime prices just rise. In other words, the performance of most commodities is very linked to economic conditions – **commodities tend to perform well when inflation is rising - when other assets like stocks or even bonds are doing poorly. In fact, commodities are the only assets, other than holding cash in a short-term savings account, that have historically consistently shown a positive return when stocks and bonds have had a negative return. This makes them very useful for diversification purposes – they compensate for the negative performance of other assets, as we shall see in more detail later. That is the main reason that we should aim to have some savings in commodities if possible.**

After commodity prices have risen, because over the slightly longer term it is usually very easy to build new capacity to produce commodities, the quantity that is available to be sold increases, and prices usually fall back down. For many non-precious commodities, a key factor that impacts their price longer-term price is the cost of getting them out of the ground, and this cost has been falling constantly over time as new technologies have been developed. Gold and silver have some useful application in manufacturing, but often are just sought out by investors because they represent real assets during periods of uncertainty; after the period of uncertainty has passed, prices usually fall back down. Oil prices often rise during periods of unrest in regions such as the Middle East where a lot of oil comes from.

**For many years, investors have believed that it is impossible to make money in commodities over the long term.** The average annual return for commodities since the 1970s has been around 3% - not very high. Accordingly there was an underinvestment in commodities for a very long time (a lot of investment was focused on the technology sector where returns have been better). Probably because of this underinvestment, recently the returns have improved for commodity investors, demonstrating once again that following the herd is not always a great way to make money.

The price of a commodity is often higher today than it is expected to be in the future. Having oil today is very valuable if you are running a refinery and do not want to shut it down – you need the commodity today to keep the refinery running. The difference between the price for oil delivered today and the price of oil delivered in one month can also be a source of return for sophisticated commodity traders.

**Many investors think of investing in commodities as investing in companies that are involved in the manufacture and/or distribution of commodities, such as oil companies.** For many of us, owning commodity related equities might be the only way unfortunately to get exposure to commodities, because commodities can be difficult to invest in. It is worth bearing in mind however that the performance of these equities depends on the performance of the companies as per their income statements, balance sheets and cash flow statements, which would depend on commodity prices, but also on many other things including the level of competition, the decisions that management takes, and the company's expenses. The performance of these equities would also depend on the flows into equities or out of equities. Investing in companies that are involved in the commodity business unfortunately does not provide as much of a diversification benefit as investing in the commodities themselves. Commodity stocks should however be a part of a diversified stock portfolio (and would of course also be included in typical major market indices like the S&P 500). In order to benefit from the diversification benefits that the underlying commodities provide, a small percentage such as 5-10% of an overall investment portfolio is typically considered enough to provide the diversification element.

<u>**Key questions that we can answer on after reading this section**</u>
**(Check that you can):**

1. What are commodities?
2. When do commodity prices usually rise?
3. Which characteristic of commodities makes them interesting as investments?

**(The answers can be easily found in this section)**

## 7.   OTHER INVESTMENTS

**When it comes to making other investments, especially those that appear to be too good to be true, the main thing to bear in mind is the Wall Street expression that 'there is no free lunch'.** Investments that appear too good to be true, in reality often are. Either they are complete scams, and one will never get any money back, or there are things that might not be immediately apparent that affect how we should think about these investments.

**For example, some banks offer capital-guaranteed products where an investor gets back a minimum of 100% of their investment after five years, and they benefit fully in the upside performance of a stock market index over the same time period.** Sounds great at first glance – we get our money back no matter what, and benefit from the full rise of the index in question. What is important to understand, however, is what one is giving up in this case. Stocks pay dividends and so do indices. For many indices the return per year through dividends alone is 3% or 4% per year. These capital-guaranteed products typically provide the price return of the index, but not the dividend yield. Assuming a dividend yield of 4%, dividends alone, with compounding and reinvesting the dividends back into the market (as an index fund would), would turn a $100 investment into $121.67 over five years - a return of 22%, which these capital-guaranteed products would not receive. In other words, if the market index stayed flat, the capital guaranteed product would return $100, whereas just investing in the market would have delivered a 22% return. If the market rose, for example by 5%, the capital guaranteed product would have gone up by 5%; if we had invested in the market directly, we would have received the 5% appreciation plus the roughly 22% of dividend return – investing in the market directly would still have been the better option. It is only when the market falls a lot that the capital guarantee comes out ahead. In fact, the market has to fall so much that it makes giving up the 22% dividend return worthwhile. If the market fell by 10% over five years, we would still have been better off investing in the market directly - we would have lost 10% through the price move, but we would have made roughly 22% in dividends. The market would have to fall by roughly 20% over the five years for the capital-guaranteed product to have any value; and such a poor performance over five years is quite rare. In fact, if that is something that we are worried about, and we are willing to give up so much upside (22%) to protect against, we should probably think twice about investing in this index in the first place.

In other words, these particular products, although they might sound good at first, are usually not attractive in practice, or at least we have to appreciate what the investment represents. Furthermore, these products often have very high built in hidden fees, and large penalties if we want to sell before the investment period (five years in this example) is up.

Other capital-guaranteed products offer a similar capital guarantee, but provide exposure to a basket of hedge funds. We would get some exposure to the hedge funds if their performance is positive, and 100% of our money back if the performance is poor, after a certain period, for example five years. Sounds good, but we know that if we put that money in the bank and commit to leaving it there for five years we would receive interest over those five years. We would probably get a pretty good rate of interest if the money is locked in for the full five years, which these products effectively do because of the high penalty charges for early sale. If we had put the money in the bank, and if the five-year risk free rate was at 3.5% per year, we would be getting almost 19% (1.035 multiplied by 1.035 five times) of return over the five years. In other words, the hedge funds would have to perform <u>extremely</u> well in order to compensate for this. And again these products usually have high fees built into them.

**The bottom line is that although these particular products are not scams per se, by reading the small print and by knowing that money gains interest and that stocks pay dividends, we can assess what the investment actually involves. When it comes to investing, there is usually no free lunch – if it seems to good to be true then it probably is. That does not mean that we cannot accumulate a lot of money, it just means that we have to save intelligently, understand what is going on, and think for ourselves a little bit based on knowing some very valuable financial truths. Stock and bond markets have gone up historically because of the relationship that savers can have with users of capital. Capital-guaranteed investments are usually not a good way of accumulating wealth because they do not offer the same return as the underlying investments and because they have such high fees.**

~

**In theory, one could 'invest' in anything with the hope of receiving a return, including cars, antique furniture, watches, books, dolls etc. Investments become investments if investors buy them and make money over time.**

Investments in equity including stocks, and debt including bonds, ideally create mutually beneficial transactions. Providers of capital have the opportunity to make a return, and users of capital are able to get access to funds that they need and can use to generate a return. The benefits of this structure make these transactions repeatable, and that is why these investments are so important. **Most other investments are different – they can be better thought of as places to park money, where the money does not really do anything while it is there.**

**Other often spoken about investments such as antiques, collectibles and art, for example, also have other typical characteristics:**

- *Each item is different* because of age, condition and sometimes even who has owned it. Price is often negotiated on an item-by-item basis; with stocks, one common stock of IBM is the same as another, and there are millions of identical shares;
- *The items are illiquid* because each one is different. Often there is no official market for them. Published price lists serve only as guidelines; the price an item will fetch can only really be determined by trying to sell it;
- *Their value cannot be determined by any real measure.* Beauty is in the eye of the beholder; it is difficult to determine value based on analytical objective measures. Rarity and demand play a large role.

Having said that, does it make sense to purchase a piece of art that brings pleasure to the eye and that might appreciate over time? Of course it does – most posters or pieces of art are virtually worthless as soon as they are taken from the store. But it does not, unless one is a professional or this is one's main business, make a case for making these investments the core element of a saving and investing program. Over many periods, the financial return for these items has been less than that of stocks, bonds, and in many cases even less than the rate of inflation. As the wealth of countries increases, which it has over the long term, objects of rarity and of beauty do tend to appreciate, but by exactly how much is difficult to determine. As more people in the world have money and adopt western capitalist values, and as their purchasing power increases, perhaps the value of these items can be expected to continue to rise. On the other hand, when people are cutting back on expenses, they tend to cut back first on items that are dispensable and these items can experience large swings in price. Furthermore, these items do not create the sustainable mutually beneficial provider and user of capital transactions that should always be beneficial over the long term in a well-functioning financial market; and they do not allow the principles of compounding, tax savings (which we will discuss shortly) and so on to be implemented effectively either.

<u>KEY QUESTIONS THAT WE CAN ANSWER AFTER READING THIS SECTION</u>
(CHECK THAT YOU CAN):

1. WHAT IS THE MAIN THING TO BEAR IN MIND WHEN WE HEAR ABOUT INVESTMENTS?
2. WHAT CAN BE MISSING FROM A CAPITAL-GUARANTEED PRODUCT THAT WOULD OTHERWISE PROVIDE A RETURN?
3. WHAT ARE OTHER INVESTMENTS WE CAN CONSIDER AND HOW SHOULD WE THINK ABOUT THEM?

(THE ANSWERS CAN BE EASILY FOUND IN THIS SECTION)

# Chapter IV

# THE ECONOMY

**The economy is often spoken about in the press, and as much as anything we need to understand what is being talked about.** Furthermore, the economy impacts investments - although timing our investments based on what we think the economy might do is not always that straightforward.

**The size of the economy of a country is most often measured with the** *Gross Domestic Product* **or GDP of a country** – this is the value of all the goods produced, and all of the value that is added by production, in a particular country. The countries with the largest GDPs are the countries with the largest economies, and these are currently the United States, China, Japan and India. Yearly changes in GDP are very interesting to follow because they indicate how quickly the economy of a country is growing, whether growth is slowing, or even whether an economy is shrinking.

**Labour and capital are two main inputs that affect the GDP of a country.** Typically as GDP rises, the *rate of unemployment* falls as companies employ more people to produce more goods. When the unemployment rate falls, consumers also feel better and consumer confidence often rises. With respect to capital, when GDP is growing, companies increase production, and the level at which they use their plant and equipment increases – this level of use is known as the *capacity utilisation*. The level of industrial economic activity is also quantified through *industrial production* numbers that measure the total output generated from mines and factories.

**To monitor the state of the economy various economic groups, government agencies and news groups carry out surveys.** Companies might be asked what they are planning to spend on equipment over the coming period, or whether they believe the economy is expanding or contracting. Three examples of important pieces of data that are looked at are:

- *The US ISM Survey* – a monthly survey that compares changes in various market areas on a monthly basis. A number over 50 indicates that the economy is expanding, and a number below 50 indicates that the economy is contracting;
- *The UK Index of Production* – a monthly survey that measures the volume of production of the manufacturing, mining and quarrying, and energy supply industries, in the United Kingdom. These sectors covered 21.8% of the UK economy in 2001;
- *IFO Survey (Germany)* – a monthly survey that asks approximately 10,000 companies in Germany how their businesses are performing in the current period and how they expect the business to perform in the coming period.

**Economic data allows the government to make forecasts and think about what they need to focus on; it allows central banks, which we will speak about shortly, to make sure that the economy is functioning well; and it allows companies to make budget forecasts. It can also help investors think about what will happen next.**

**As an economy grows, the prices of goods and services tend to increase slightly each year. This increase in prices is known as *inflation*.** Inflation is also sometimes described as too many dollars chasing too few goods. An annual inflation rate of 3% means that prices of goods and services are rising at 3% per year. Inflation is important because as prices rise, what we can buy each year with the same amount of money is less. The longer the time period, and the higher the rate of inflation, the more significant the impact. The following table shows how much more expensive goods would get as a result of various rates of inflation over different time periods.

| INFLATION | 10 YRS | 20 YRS | 30 YRS | 40 YRS |
|---|---|---|---|---|
| 3% | 34.39% | 80.61% | 142.73% | 226.20% |
| 4% | 48.02% | 119.11% | 224.34% | 380.10% |
| 5% | 62.89% | 165.33% | 332.19% | 604.00% |
| 6% | 79.08% | 220.71% | 474.35% | 928.57% |
| 7% | 96.72% | 286.97% | 661.23% | 1397.45% |
| 8% | 115.89% | 366.10% | 906.27% | 2072.45% |

Even with inflation of only 3%, the cost of goods appreciates substantially over a longer period of time. Very high inflation also leads to instability as prices just move up too quickly for consumers and producers to keep up. Inflation is measured by looking at indicators such as the *Producer Price Index*, which looks as prices paid to producers, and the *Consumer Price Index*, which looks at the retail prices of goods and services.

An inflation rate of 3% will raise prices by 16% over five years (1.03 multiplied by 1.03 five times) and by just over 34% over 10 years (1.03 multiplied by 1.03 ten times). Our salaries will often adjust with inflation, but money that we have saved will buy less if it does not earn at least the rate of inflation. For example, if money is kept under our pillows without earning any return, then what we can buy each year will be less. To keep the same purchasing power, we need to make sure that our money grows at least in line with inflation; to increase our spending power or increase our real wealth, our return needs to exceed inflation. This means making a *real* return. For example, if the interest rate that we receive is 5% and the rate of inflation is 2%, then the real return or the real rate of interest is:

Real Interest Rate  =  Nominal Interest Rate – Inflation

= 5% - 2% = 3%

Although interest rates are at 5%, because of inflation of 2% per year, we are only getting a real return of 3%. The 5% interest rate is known as the nominal interest rate; it is the interest rate in name – hence the word nominal. All interest rates that are given at the bank and in the press are nominal. We have to subtract inflation as above to figure out the real rate. If the nominal return is 3%, and if inflation is running at 3%, then we are effectively not getting wealthier with this return.

Inflation is prevalent - because the level of wealth tends to increase over time, because most populations are growing, and because the need for goods and services tends to grow over the long-term. An inflation rate of 2-3% is typical and is roughly the average for the United States and the United Kingdom over the last 75 years. There have also been exceptional periods of higher inflation during these 75 years due to high growth and/or supply disruptions.

Given inflation, getting a return is very important, because as we saw, even with low inflation, the impact on the price of goods is substantial over the longer term. Stocks and bonds have offered a return that is better than inflation over the past 75 years – keeping the money under a pillow where it gathers no interest, or in a savings account where it gathers very little interest, will not.

The opposite of inflation is deflation, where instead of appreciating in value, goods get cheaper. Deflation often comes after major market corrections where people have lost significant amounts of money. Goods and services need to get cheaper in order to become affordable again. If we have a lot of debt, deflation can be a big problem because unfortunately debt does not *deflate* in the same way as our assets will. Let's think back to our balance sheet - if the value of our assets goes down because of deflation, and our debt stays the same or grows, then in order to balance, the value of our equity has to drop in a leveraged manner - faster than the assets are falling in value. Fortunately, deflation is less common than inflation.

**Because inflation, and to some extent deflation (although it is less common), can affect purchasing power so dramatically, and because the two can lead to difficulties in monitoring prices if the rates of change are very high, most countries have a central bank which has as its main task keeping inflation under control.** The central bank is the bank of the country, and of the economy as a whole, and it acts with the government, although it is often independent of the government, to ensure that inflation is kept in check and that the economy and the financial system of a country or region are functioning well. The central bank is also usually responsible for issuing currency and printing money, setting short-term interest rates, regulating the banking system and in some cases providing banking services to the government and other financial institutions.

**The United States, Canada, the United Kingdom all have central banks** - the Federal Reserve Bank in the US, the Bank of Canada in Canada, and the Bank of England in the United Kingdom. Because the countries of the European Union form one economic region, there is one European Central Bank (ECB). Economic stability and low and stable inflation are the primary objectives of these central banks. Sometimes currency considerations also play a role - currency strength can affect a country's competitiveness, and interest rates can contribute to currency strength. Teams of economists at central banks monitor the economy through the data and surveys that are available, and they also investigate important economic topics themselves. Most importantly the central banks take decisions to make sure that its objectives for inflation and growth are worked towards.

**If the central bank comes to the conclusion that growth is too fast and/or inflation is a risk, it adjusts *monetary policy* either by changing interest rates, or by changing the amount of money in circulation in the economy.** Changing interest rates is the most significant mechanism by which central banks influence the growth of the economy and inflation. The central bank sets the interest rate that other banks or major private sector institutions have to pay when they borrow money overnight. This rate is a benchmark for other interest rates, and ultimately trickles through the economy and causes banks to adjust the rates at which consumers and businesses can borrow. Anyone that relies on debt as a source of funding realises that the cost of financing has gone up when the central bank raises interest rates. Faced with a higher interest cost, companies and consumers typically adjust their spending down and the overall economy begins to slow, easing the pressure on inflation.

Central banks also make statements regarding the economy and hint at where they think that interest rates might go in the future. This is important because these statements will affect longer-term risk-free rates. According to the expectations theory, the longer-term is a product of all of the shorter time periods between now and the longer-term. For example, a two-year interest rate is [1 + the one-year rate] *multiplied by* [1 + the one year rate, one year from now] annualised to give a percentage; the three year rate is [1+the one-year rate] multiplied by [1 + the one-year rate, one year from now] multiplied by [1 + the one-year rate, two years from now] annualised to give a percentage, or alternatively [1 + the two-year rate] multiplied by [1 + the one-year rate, two years from now] annualised to give a percentage and so on.

If the central bank says that inflation pressure is expected to rise and that they will need to make adjustments in the future that are more aggressive than people expect, short-term interest rates would be expected to rise in the future and therefore longer-term rates would rise today. As these longer-term interest rates rise, borrowing costs also rise and the economy would also typically slow as companies and consumers borrow less. As these longer-term risk-free rates rise, bond prices would also fall with the higher required rate of return.

In conducting monetary policy, the central bank can also issue, or buy back, government bonds to alter the amount of 'spendable' cash in the financial system. If the central bank sells bonds, individuals, companies and banks use cash to buy the bonds and cash is taken out of circulation. Less money means less spending, less demand and lower inflation. If the central bank buys bonds in the market, it releases cash back into the economy, thereby increasing the money supply.

Some central banks including the Federal Reserve Bank in the United States (the 'Fed') also set a required reserve ratio, which is the percentage of their customers' deposits that commercial banks are required to hold at the central bank. It is money that the commercial bank cannot lend out. By lowering the required reserve ratio, commercial banks can lend out more money that then flows into the economy. To reduce inflation, the central bank can raise the required reserve ratio, thereby leaving less money for lending purposes and taking money out of the economy.

**When an economy slows, it often slows for too long, or too much, resulting in too much capacity and not enough demand** - companies might begin to reduce prices, cut back production, and lay off workers. Laying off workers influences consumer confidence and consumer demand. As all of this happens, growth slows; if prices are reduced, the inflation pressure is eliminated by definition. To stimulate the economy, the central bank could loosen monetary policy by lowering interest rates, reducing interest expenses and putting money back into the economy that can be spent. Growth should pick up as companies show better profits with lower interest expenses, as companies can borrow more cheaply to invest, and with the better profits, perhaps begin thinking about investing and hiring people. Consumers would also be able to borrow more cheaply and be stimulated to spend more. Ultimately, inflationary signs might reappear, and interest rates might once again be raised to counter this pressure.

**We can see how the whole process is cyclical** - the process of growth, inflation pressure, interest rate hikes, slowdown and interest rate cuts repeats itself in general terms over and over again. That is why *economic cycles* are often spoken about. Sometimes periods of growth are longer because there are no signs of inflation, sometimes the downturn is more severe or prolonged, sometimes only certain parts of the economy are affected, and often the situation is slightly more complex – but in general terms, the same thing happens over and over again.

**Ideally of course central banks would like to keep the economy in the perfect sweet spot of moderate inflation and good growth.** That is what would make consumers, businesses and the government the happiest, and it would avoid these economic cycles entirely. Unfortunately this is difficult to do. First of all, the central bank will use its tools based on the data and analysis that it has available, and sometimes different pieces of economic data can be slightly inconsistent. Furthermore, no one knows exactly what will happen in the future, which is where the changes that the central bank makes will have impact. Economic data about the past and present is easy to get, but forecasts for the future always come with uncertainty. Furthermore, when things are going well, in many industries, companies often overbuild capacity to go for available market share – taking the future impact of this into account can be difficult. International trade also connects the economies of many regions to such an extent, that any individual central bank cannot account for the impact of what is going to happen in another region exactly. The Bank of England or the Federal Reserve Bank might be right on target, but if there is a massive crisis in a certain region or very strong growth in another region, their efforts may not yield the exact desired results. So economic cycles are here to stay, although over time, central banks have become better at gauging the state of the economy and at making their interventions more precise. Nonetheless there is a constant feedback mechanism of adjustments, monitoring what is happening, adjusting, monitoring and so on.

We know that stocks and bonds can be valued based on the future cash flows that they provide. These future benefits and their value today will be affected by the economy – growth, interest rates or the risk-free rate and so on. As we know, active management of stocks and bonds is challenging because we never know exactly what will happen in the future; nonetheless, we can say that, in general, economic theory would lead us to believe the following:

- ***Strong growth and high capacity utilisations should be good for companies all other things being equal.*** Demand for their products should be strong, they should have more power to set prices where they want to, and profits should be good. Strong growth and strong consumer confidence should be best for companies that sell consumer goods; strong industrial production and strong capital expenditure should be best for industrial companies as they see more demand for their products;

- ***Strong growth should be good for real estate and commodity investments.*** Real estate investments should rise as people have more money and feel good about the future. Commodity prices should rise as there is stronger demand for these products when economic growth picks up;

- ***Rising interest rates or expectations of rising interest rates are generally bad for investments, because it means that the risk-free rate and therefore the required rate of return that we divide by is rising.*** Today's value of future cash flows will be less. This is definitely the case for low-risk bonds, where cash flows are well defined. Because periods of rising interest rates often coincide with strong economic growth and growth in earnings, the impact on stocks will depend upon which effect is stronger – the higher earnings or the potentially higher required rate of return;

- ***Falling interest rates are generally good for investments implying a lower required rate of return and a higher present value of future cash flows.*** This is definitely the case for low-risk bonds where future cash flows are well defined. In the case of stocks, falling interest rates often coincide with weak growth and perhaps weak earnings; and again the question becomes which effect is stronger, the weaker earnings, or the potentially lower required rate of return. If earnings and cash flows to shareholders are strong and interest rates are falling, then this should be good for stock prices.

**At times monetary policy has less of an effect on investments than we would expect.** Sometimes, after very long periods of expansion, there is so much excess productive capacity, that it takes a long period of restructuring to get back to a situation where companies have an opportunity to make money. The issues affecting the economy in this case are more specific to industries than to interest rates and monetary policy.

**Aside from the monetary policy that is set by the central bank, every country also has a *fiscal policy*, which is set by the government.** Fiscal policy is the policy of government spending and taxation. If the government is spending more than it is receiving, it is said to be running a *deficit*. A government that is running a deficit will need to borrow more money in the bond market than it otherwise would. With this deficit, the government's debt would increase, and at some point in the future they would be expected to repay this debt to all of the bondholders that bought it.

Fiscal policy is also important because it can affect the economy. Taxes for companies, known as corporate taxes, affect company spending. Income taxes and other consumer taxes affect how we as consumers spend. How companies and consumers are taxed, and what the government spends on parts of the economy, clearly affects growth, inflation and ultimately the overall economy. If the government raises taxes for companies and individuals, both have less money to spend, and growth and inflation should decrease. When taxes are lowered, parts of the economy might receive a boost because companies and/or individuals have more money to spend. Therefore the fiscal and monetary policies in a country need to be coordinated. When the government implements tax changes, the central bank will be sure to monitor the impact of these changes to ensure that the policy goals of low and stable inflation and a well functioning economy continue to be met.

KEY QUESTIONS THAT WE CAN ANSWER AFTER READING THIS SECTION
(CHECK THAT YOU CAN):

1.  HOW ARE THE SIZE OF AN ECONOMY AND THE GROWTH OF AN
    ECONOMY MEASURED?
2.  WHAT ARE SOME OF THE MAIN ECONOMIC INDICATORS AND PIECES OF
    DATA THAT ARE LOOKED AT?
3.  WHAT IS INFLATION AND WHY IS IT IMPORTANT?
4.  WHAT IS A REAL RETURN?
5.  WHAT IS A CENTRAL BANK AND WHAT IS ITS ROLE?
6.  HOW DOES THE CENTRAL BANK AFFECT INTEREST RATES?
7.  WHAT DOES THE EXPECTATIONS THEORY SAY ABOUT LONGER-TERM
    RATES?
8.  WHY ARE ECONOMIC CYCLES HERE TO STAY?
9.  WHAT CAN WE SAY ABOUT THE ECONOMY AND INVESTMENTS?
10. WHAT IS A FISCAL POLICY?

(THE ANSWERS CAN BE EASILY FOUND IN THIS CHAPTER)

**Chapter V**

# Saving And Investing In Practice

We have learned almost all we need to know – about compounding, debt, equity, financial markets, investments and the economy. But before we can get started there are a few very important practical considerations we need to be aware of.

## I. The Impact of Time

History has shown that that the value of good companies, and that the value of the stock market as a whole, have risen over time, probably in large part because of the mutually beneficial relationship that providers and users of capital can have. The returns of the stock market over any one-year period however, go up and down quite a bit in what seems like a random pattern. Companies go bankrupt and disappear, others are created, the economy might shrink - over any one-year period the returns are quite volatile.

The movement or volatility in the returns can be illustrated by looking at the returns of the S&P 500 index from year to year. Again we will use this index because it is the one for which data is most easily available for a long period of time. We could equally use the return for the FTSE 100 or another developed country stock market index – the results and conclusions would be similar.

As an investor in equities, we know that our total return will be made up of the return from the price change, also known as the capital appreciation, and the additional return from dividends. If we look at the returns for the last sixty-five years, the annual total percentage returns would look like this:

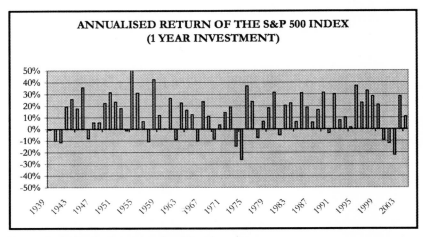

*Source: Author's calculations based on Bloomberg data.*

As we can see, the returns vary a great deal between the years. For example, money invested it the S&P 500 in at the end of 1938 would have been down .5% in the first year (1939); in the next year it would have fallen by 9.7%; and then we would have lost another 11.2% the year after. Money that was invested at the beginning of 1939 would have lost over 20% of its value by the beginning of 1942. On the graph, we can see how the returns jump around a lot, and how they were in fact negative, and even significantly negative, in numerous years. Over this period, the return (including dividends) was negative more than one quarter of the time (17 out of 65 years), and low in many other years. Since we cannot time the market, the risk of losing money in any given year if we had invested for one year during this period, would have been quite high. **If we had invested for a shorter period and not collected all of the dividends that are paid out over the year, the risk of losing money would have been even higher.**

Now let's look at what happens if instead of looking at the returns for one year, we look at an investment that is kept in the S&P 500 index for a longer period of time, for example three years. If we had invested at the beginning of 1939, and left the investment in place for 3 years, we would have lost .46% in the first year, 9.71% in the second year and 11.15% in the third year. Over the three-year period we would have lost 20.15% of our money. In the next three-year period we would have lost 9.71% in the first year, lost 11.15% in the second year, and made 19.22% in the third year. This equivalent to losing 4.37% over these three years. We can continue, and calculate what the return would have been for each three-year period.

**As we can see from the table on the next page, the three-year return is positive much more often than the one-year return.** In other words, if we had invested for three year periods, the return would have been positive much more often.

From this three-year return we can calculate an equivalent annual return. This is the return that if we had earned it for each of the three years, would give the return of the three year period. This return is labeled the '3 YR ANN RETURN'.

**For example, for the period ending in 1941, this average return is the return that if we lost it in each of the three years, would be the same as losing 20.15% over the three years.** This return is:

$$((100\% - 20.15\%)^{1/3} - 1) \times 100\% = -7.23\%$$

Losing 7.23% each year for three years is equivalent to losing 20.15% over three years. To check this we can start at 100 and say that after the first year we would be at:

$$100 * (100\% - 7.23\%) \quad = 92.77$$

After the second year we would have:

$$92.77 * (100\% - 7.23\%) = 86.07$$

After the third year we would have:

$$86.07 * (100 - 7.23\%) \quad = 79.85$$

An investment that goes from 100 to 79.85 has lost <u>20.15%</u> of its value ((100-79.85)/100) as above, and this confirms that losing 7.23% each year for three years is the same as losing 20.15% over three years (and the same as losing .46% in the first year, 9.71% in the second year, and 11.15% in the third year). The -7.23% is the equivalent annualised return for this three-year period.

We can calculate the three year return and the equivalent annualised return for each three-year period for the S&P 500. For the 25 years from 1939 to 1964, this looks like this:

| YEAR | S&P 500 LEVEL | DIVIDENDS | 1 YEAR RETURN | 3 YEAR RETURN | 3 YR ANN RETURN |
|------|------|------|------|------|------|
| 1939 | 17.66 | 0.62 | -0.46% | | |
| 1940 | 24.35 | 0.67 | -9.71% | | |
| 1941 | 21.45 | 0.71 | -11.15% | -20.15% | -7.23% |
| 1942 | 15.34 | 0.59 | 19.22% | -4.37% | -1.48% |
| 1943 | 8.12 | 0.61 | 25.69% | 33.13% | 10.01% |
| 1945 | 6.92 | 0.44 | 17.57% | 76.17% | 20.77% |
| 1946 | 9.97 | 0.66 | 35.69% | 100.51% | 26.10% |
| 1947 | 9.50 | 0.71 | -7.78% | 47.12% | 13.73% |
| 1948 | 13.43 | 0.84 | 5.49% | 32.01% | 9.70% |
| 1949 | 17.18 | 0.93 | 5.42% | 2.56% | 0.85% |
| 1950 | 10.55 | 1.80 | 22.30% | 36.02% | 10.80% |
| 1951 | 13.14 | 1.64 | 31.45% | 69.48% | 19.23% |
| 1952 | 12.46 | 1.41 | 23.25% | 98.14% | 25.60% |
| 1953 | 10.58 | 1.41 | 17.71% | 90.70% | 24.01% |
| 1954 | 8.69 | 1.45 | -1.17% | 43.39% | 12.76% |
| 1955 | 9.77 | 1.54 | 51.23% | 75.94% | 20.72% |
| 1956 | 11.67 | 1.64 | 30.96% | 95.74% | 25.09% |
| 1957 | 13.28 | 1.74 | 6.44% | 110.81% | 28.22% |
| 1958 | 17.36 | 1.79 | -10.48% | 24.79% | 7.66% |
| 1959 | 15.30 | 1.75 | 42.44% | 35.73% | 10.72% |
| 1960 | 15.30 | 1.83 | 11.79% | 42.55% | 12.54% |
| 1961 | 15.20 | 1.95 | 0.28% | 59.68% | 16.88% |
| 1962 | 16.79 | 2.02 | 26.60% | 41.93% | 12.38% |
| 1963 | 20.43 | 2.13 | -8.83% | 15.75% | 5.00% |
| 1964 | 23.77 | 2.28 | 22.50% | 41.40% | 12.24% |

*Source: Author's calculations based on Bloomberg data; the 1 Year Return is a slight approximation because the dividend payments are spread throughout the year.*

In each case, the three-year annualised return is the equivalent annual return that we would get if we left the money invested for three years. If we had invested for three years ending in 1942, the average annual return would have been -1.48%, (which is equivalent to a having had returns of –9.71%, -11.15% and +19.22%). If we had invested for the three years ending in 1943, our equivalent annualised return would have been +10.01% and so on.

**When we plot this annualised three-year return, we can see that in contrast to the one-year return, it jumps around a lot less. In other words, if the money is invested for three years, the average yearly return is less volatile and more likely to end up being positive.**

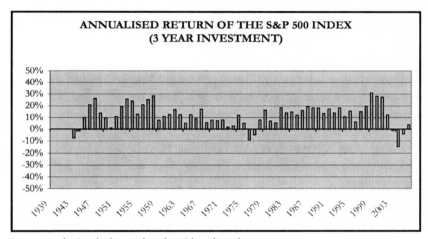

*Source: Author's calculations based on Bloomberg data.*

We can do the same thing assuming that we had invested for five years and calculate the annualized return for a five-year period. This 'average' annual return that we would have received if we had invested in the S&P 500 index for five years looks as shown in the next chart.

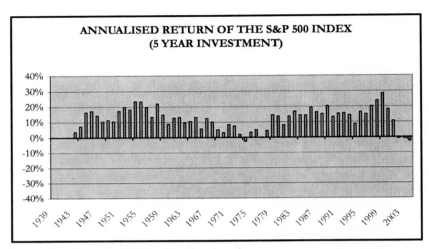

*Source: Author's calculations based on Bloomberg data.*

**For a five-year investment the 'average' return jumps around even less - there are a lot of annual returns bunched between 10% and 20%, and even more returns are positive.**

Let's look at what happens when we look at a 10-year period – the average annual returns that would have been obtained if we had invested in the S&P 500 for ten years.

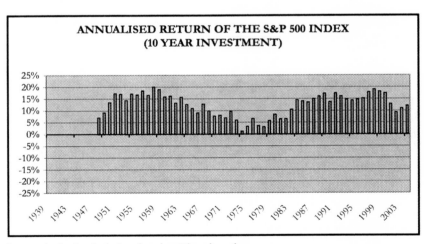

*Source: Author's calculations based on Bloomberg data.*

Let's look at the 'average' annual return that we would obtain if the investment were left in place for twenty years.

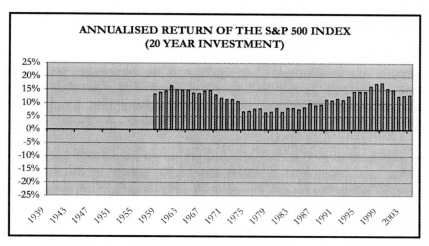

Source: Author's calculations based on Bloomberg data.

And finally, let's look at the 'average' annual return that we would obtain if the investment were left in place for thirty years.

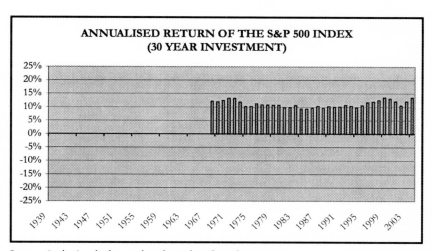

Source: Author's calculations based on Bloomberg data.

As we can see, as the investment is left in place for longer and longer periods of time, the less the returns move around, and the more the average annual returns are bunched up in the range of 10-15%. The longer the period, the more averaging takes place.

In practice this means that, in order to capture positive long-term returns from a volatile asset like equities, it has been easier to predict the result when the asset is held for a long time. Over short time periods the returns are very difficult to predict, and jump around a lot. A longer time horizon significantly increases the likelihood of having a good result.

One implication of this is that when we invest in volatile assets like equities, our investment horizon should be longer to increase our chances of achieving a positive result. In other words, if we have a very long time horizon, the volatile movements of the equity market in each year are not as much of a concern if we believe that the investment will rise over the long term, which it has very successfully over history as we can see. That is why it is often said that the younger the saver, the higher the percentage of savings that can be allocated to equities – by the time the money is needed, thirty or forty years might have passed and the year to year fluctuations would have become much less relevant. On the other hand, if we know that we will need the money in one or two years, and can't afford a potential big loss, or want to be more sure of a positive return, less volatile assets such as debt investments are much more suitable even though they have historically offered a lower return - the shorter the maturity, and the lower the risk, the less volatile the debt investment will be.

KEY QUESTIONS THAT WE CAN ANSWER AFTER READING THIS SECTION (CHECK THAT YOU CAN):

1. HOW CAN WE REDUCE THE VOLATILITY OF OUR AVERAGE RETURN FOR AN EQUITY INVESTMENT?
2. WHAT DOES THIS IMPLY FOR HOW LONG WE SHOULD THINK ABOUT INVESTING IN EQUITY ASSETS?
3. WHAT DOES THAT MEAN FOR WHEN WE WANT TO INVEST FOR A SHORTER TIME PERIOD?

(THE ANSWERS CAN BE EASILY FOUND IN THIS SECTION)

## 2.   TIMING INVESTMENTS AND DOLLAR COST AVERAGING

**One of the biggest reasons that investors do not achieve the returns that they could is that they do not recognise the implications of the short-term volatility of investments given the charts of the last section.** Furthermore, since we cannot time the market, even if we invest after a period of poor performance, we cannot be sure that this is a good idea, since we do not know what will happen in the future. The whole thing is complicated further by the fact that human nature is such that we are often tempted to try to time the market by putting more money into the market after a period of positive performance, in order to capture more returns, or to throw in the towel and sell investments after a period of very poor performance.

**Being aware of investor behaviour is useful in understanding some of the pitfalls that we might fall into. For example, investor behaviour in the short term is often influenced by headlines such as: 'the real estate market is hot and expected to go higher', 'stocks are performing well and should continue to rally' splashed across the front pages of the newspaper.** When we hear things like this, we should always think about what this means in terms of the expectations that investors have. If everyone thinks real estate is going higher, then probably either sellers would wait to sell, or they would sell at a higher price today reflecting the fact that they think the asset will be more expensive soon. Buyers, would probably be prepared to pay higher prices today as well, for fear of having to pay more soon. Therefore the expectation of higher prices often means that prices are already high. This does not leave much room for the good news to impact prices positively in the short term. The good news will already be in the price, and when good news does come out, the asset price might not even go up because it was so widely expected. If anything, very positive expectations leave room for disappointment – disappointments that cause asset prices to drop dramatically when everyone has been anticipating good news. Conversely, if everyone thinks that an investment will continue to go down, expectations might be so low that negative news will no longer impact the price of the investment, and positive news will cause a very positive stock price reaction.

**Given the role of expectations, smart investors spend a lot of time trying to figure out things that might be unexpected by the majority of investors.** In the stock market, they try to think about things that are not on the front page of the newspaper and that might not be reflected in prices. In the real estate market, they might look for well-located properties in an overlooked area that would probably have more potential than properties in an area that everyone is focused on, certainly in the short-term. It is worth bearing expectations in mind, especially when assessing what the short-term performance might be, or whether going with the crowd blindly is a good idea.

**Throughout history, situations have arisen where investors got caught up in frenzies and blindly expected positive performance to continue. Looking back on this now, it seems that the only reason investors could have justified buying the investments is because they thought that they could be resold at a higher price in the future to someone else that was caught up in the frenzy.** Neither the price at which they bought the investment, nor the higher price at which they expected to sell it at, appear linked to the value of the item. This is sometimes referred to as the *greater fool theory* – investors expect a 'greater fool' to purchase the investment from them. At some point investors come to their senses and become aware of the discrepancy between the price of the asset and its true value. The bubble bursts as buyers disappear and sellers are unable to sell; since prices are often so far above real values, they can fall significantly and quickly. Extreme examples of this include:

- The share prices of technology companies in the 1990s. Valuing stocks as it had been done up until then was largely ignored or revised. It was argued that things were different this time and that traditional valuation models were no longer relevant. Unfortunately for many, the same old valuation methods soon became relevant again and prices began to drop. When prices began to drop, there was no reason left to buy the stocks – why buy a stock that is not going up and that doesn't look cheap? Many companies lost more than 90% of their value over the twelve months that followed March 2000;
- The Nikkei stock index in Japan in the 1980s, which went from roughly 9,900 in 1983 to 39,000 by the end of 1989, a four-fold rise in 6 years, or a return of 26% percent compounded for each of the six years. In 1990 it crashed back to 24,000. During the same bubble period, the price of real estate in Japan ballooned so high that the real estate of Japan, a country that fits into the United States approximately 25 times, was worth four times that of the US. When it became apparent that true values could not support these prices, the price of land in Japan came crashing down as well;
- Tulip prices in the 1630s, which rose so high that the price of a tulip was measured in terms of cows, pigs, land and even houses. Prices in no way reflected the benefits of tulips. Speculators had no real interest

in owning the tulips except for speculation purposes - once prices began to drop, there was a mad rush to sell them. The price of tulips eventually dropped to a mere fraction of the previous price.

**Perhaps because of the fear of missing a good thing,** *bubbles* **like this appear again and and again, and smart people get caught up in them. As savers and investors, common sense and keeping an eye on the fundamental or true value is always a good idea.**

**Outside of valuation and the greater fool theory, there are other factors that can affect how we think about investments.** Costs that have been incurred in the past and that cannot be recovered should not impact our decision-making process – these costs are known as *sunk costs*. If someone bought a house ten years ago, should the price at which they bought it at impact their decision to keep it or sell it? The answer is no – the only thing that matters is what the future benefits are and what someone might be willing to pay for the item today, or in the future when it is going to be sold. The key to valuation is looking at the future benefits and cash flows that assets provide, not things that have happened in the past.

**Related to the concept of sunk cost, is** *loss aversion* **- an aversion, or a dislike, for taking losses.** Sometimes remembering an item's original price, leads us to avoid selling the item if it means taking a loss. Again, the past should not affect our decision to keep or to sell a bought item. If someone bought a house for $100,000 and the value went to $90,000, from a financial standpoint, whether it makes sense to sell it depends on the likelihood of it going up or down in the future, not what the resulting loss would be today. The same thing is true for stocks and bonds – it is difficult to sell stocks that have gone from $90 to $30 because of the loss that would be realised, but whether it is a good idea to own a stock now, should have nothing to do with the original price, and everything to do with what is likely to happen in the future. (Tax considerations sometimes play a role when it comes to taking losses against gains, but the point here is about anchoring oneself to a price that is no longer relevant).

**Another mental process that takes place is mental accounting.** Mental accounting refers to giving different values to money depending on where it came from. For many people a $10 bill found in the street has a different value than $10 earned through hard work - it is much easier to turn around and spend the $10 that was just found on the street, than it is to spend the $10 earned through hard work. Mental accounting also explains why someone would be willing to look at a number of stores to save $10 on a $50 radio, whereas one might be much less likely to make the same effort to save $10 on a $500 television. People tend not to pay as much attention to each dollar spent when making large purchases. Clearly, ten dollars is ten dollars, no matter where it comes from. Mental accounting can ultimately lead to a series of small losses that will with time add up to a large amount.

**The mental processes that go on are interesting to bear in mind when we think about our finances. Despite what many of us might think, these things that do not appear logical, occur over and over again to smart savers and investors. Seeing what is happening while it is happening is much more difficult than reviewing it once it has happened, so we should bear these traps in mind.**

**When it comes to saving money, any amount saved can be very important, especially given the power of compounding. Furthermore, we cannot time the market but will often be tempted to.** Therefore, one of the best things for us to do is to automate a part of our investing process. A method that works very well, and that we should use, is known as dollar cost averaging (or pound cost averaging in the UK). It involves investing the same amount of money, for example $200, on a regular basis, no matter what the price of the asset is. As the price of what is being bought goes up and down, the quantity bought will vary - more will be bought when prices are low, and less will be bought when prices are high. This leads to a lower average price, as we shall see.

For example, if we invest $200 in each of two months, with the stock price in the first month being $10 and in the second month being $20, after two months we would have invested $400, and bought 20 stocks in the first month and 10 stocks (for $200) in the second month for a total of 30 stocks bought over the two months. This means that the average price that we paid for the stocks bought would be $13.33 ($400/30). But if we calculated the average price over the two months, without having averaged our investment, it would have been $15 (($10+$20)/2). Because we invested the same amount each month, we bought more at lower prices and less at higher prices, and the average price was lowered significantly!

Let's see how this might work in practice with an investor who invests $100 each month irrespective of a stock's price, assuming that we can buy partial shares, which is often possible. The table below shows the investment, the stock price, the number of shares bought, the number of stocks owned at each point in time, the total investment so far at each point in time and the average price of the stocks that have been purchased to date.

| MONTH | INVESTMENT | STOCK PRICE | STOCKS BOUGHT | STOCKS OWNED | AMOUNT INVESTED | AVERAGE PRICE |
|---|---|---|---|---|---|---|
| 1 | $100.00 | $20.00 | 5.00 | 5 | $100.00 | $20.00 |
| 2 | $100.00 | $21.00 | 4.76 | 9.76 | $200.00 | $20.49 |
| 3 | $100.00 | $22.00 | 4.55 | 14.31 | $300.00 | $20.97 |
| 4 | $100.00 | $23.00 | 4.35 | 18.66 | $400.00 | $21.44 |
| 5 | $100.00 | $21.00 | 4.76 | 23.42 | $500.00 | $21.35 |
| 6 | $100.00 | $19.00 | 5.26 | 28.68 | $600.00 | $20.92 |
| 7 | $100.00 | $18.00 | 5.56 | 34.24 | $700.00 | $20.45 |
| 8 | $100.00 | $17.00 | 5.88 | 40.12 | $800.00 | $19.94 |
| 9 | $100.00 | $16.00 | 6.25 | 46.37 | $900.00 | $19.41 |
| 10 | $100.00 | $15.00 | 6.67 | 53.03 | $1,000.00 | $18.86 |
| 11 | $100.00 | $18.00 | 5.56 | 58.59 | $1,100.00 | $18.77 |
| 12 | $100.00 | $22.00 | 4.55 | 63.14 | $1,200.00 | $19.01 |

In the first month, the stock price was $20, and 5 shares were bought. As the price went up, fewer shares were bought with the same amount of money (i.e. 4.76 shares in month 2). When the price went down, more shares were bought. At the end of 12 months, 63.14 shares had been bought with an investment of $1,200 so the average price was ($1,200/63.14 = $19.01). This compares with the regular average price over that same period which is:

$$= \frac{(20+21+22+23+21+19+18+17+16+15+18+22)}{12} = \$19.33$$

By investing the same amount of money to buy more when prices were low, and less when prices were high, we are again able to reduce our average purchase price significantly!

**Over the long term, when investing in even more volatile assets, the reduction in purchase price that can be achieved by dollar cost averaging becomes even more noteworthy.** Let's assume that someone had been putting $2,000 at the end of each year between 1975 and 2004 (thirty years) into an S&P 500 index fund - a fund that costs exactly the same amount as the level of the S&P 500. We have already seen that this equity index, as most do, moves around a lot on a yearly basis; furthermore we know that index funds are a great product for investors.

In 1975, the investor would have bought: $2000/90.19 = 22.18 units. In 1976 he or she would have bought 18.61 units, and so on - each year additional units are bought with the $2,000 investments.

| YEAR | S&P 500 | UNITS BOUGHT | UNITS HELD | AMOUNT INVESTED | AVERAGE PRICE |
|------|---------|--------------|------------|-----------------|---------------|
| 1975 | 90.19 | 22.18 | 22.18 | $2,000.00 | $90.19 |
| 1976 | 107.46 | 18.61 | 40.79 | $4,000.00 | $98.07 |
| 1977 | 95.10 | 21.03 | 61.82 | $6,000.00 | $97.06 |
| 1978 | 96.11 | 20.81 | 82.63 | $8,000.00 | $96.82 |
| 1979 | 107.94 | 18.53 | 101.16 | $10,000.00 | $98.86 |
| 1980 | 135.76 | 14.73 | 115.89 | $12,000.00 | $103.55 |
| 1981 | 122.55 | 16.32 | 132.21 | $14,000.00 | $105.89 |
| 1982 | 140.64 | 14.22 | 146.43 | $16,000.00 | $109.27 |
| 1983 | 164.93 | 12.13 | 158.55 | $18,000.00 | $113.53 |
| 1984 | 167.24 | 11.96 | 170.51 | $20,000.00 | $117.29 |
| 1985 | 211.28 | 9.47 | 179.98 | $22,000.00 | $122.24 |
| 1986 | 242.17 | 8.26 | 188.24 | $24,000.00 | $127.50 |
| 1987 | 247.08 | 8.09 | 196.33 | $26,000.00 | $132.43 |
| 1988 | 277.72 | 7.20 | 203.53 | $28,000.00 | $137.57 |
| 1989 | 353.40 | 5.66 | 209.19 | $30,000.00 | $143.41 |
| 1990 | 330.22 | 6.06 | 215.25 | $32,000.00 | $148.66 |
| 1991 | 417.09 | 4.80 | 220.05 | $34,000.00 | $154.51 |
| 1992 | 435.71 | 4.59 | 224.64 | $36,000.00 | $160.26 |
| 1993 | 466.45 | 4.29 | 228.92 | $38,000.00 | $165.99 |
| 1994 | 459.27 | 4.35 | 233.28 | $40,000.00 | $171.47 |
| 1995 | 615.93 | 3.25 | 236.53 | $42,000.00 | $177.57 |
| 1996 | 740.74 | 2.70 | 239.23 | $44,000.00 | $183.93 |
| 1997 | 970.43 | 2.06 | 241.29 | $46,000.00 | $190.65 |
| 1998 | 1229.23 | 1.63 | 242.91 | $48,000.00 | $197.60 |
| 1999 | 1469.25 | 1.36 | 244.27 | $50,000.00 | $204.69 |
| 2000 | 1320.28 | 1.51 | 245.79 | $52,000.00 | $211.56 |
| 2001 | 1148.08 | 1.74 | 247.53 | $54,000.00 | $218.15 |
| 2002 | 879.82 | 2.27 | 249.80 | $56,000.00 | $224.18 |
| 2003 | 1111.92 | 1.80 | 251.60 | $58,000.00 | $230.52 |
| 2004 | 1211.92 | 1.65 | 253.25 | $60,000.00 | $236.92 |

The average price paid for the units is $236.92 over the thirty-year period, compared to the straight yearly average of the S&P 500 over this period, which is 512.20 (the sum of all the Indexes from 1975-2004, divided by 30). By buying more shares at lower prices, the average price is significantly lowered.

By investing $60,000 in total, the investor ended up with 253.25 units, each worth $1,211.92, and the portfolio has a value of 253.25 x $1,211.92 = $306,922.73, having invested a sum of only $60,000. The return would have actually been even greater because we would have also received dividends.

**Dollar cost averaging helps keep the average purchase price down, and when we compound over long periods of time, has a tremendous impact on the final amount of money saved. By buying more units at lower prices, and less at higher ones, dollar cost averaging is a very powerful way to increase returns over the long term. By automating the investment process, dollar cost averaging also helps us avoid falling into some of the traps that human nature would otherwise let us fall into.**

<u>KEY QUESTIONS THAT WE CAN ANSWER AFTER READING THIS SECTION</u>
(CHECK THAT YOU CAN):

1. WHAT ROLE DO EXPECTATIONS PLAY IN ESTABLISHING THE PRICE OF INVESTMENTS?
2. WHAT ARE BUBBLES?
3. WHAT ARE SOME OF THE MENTAL PROCESSES THAT MIGHT LEAD US TO MAKING IRRATIONAL DECISIONS?
4. HOW CAN WE AVOID LETTING EMOTIONS DRIVE OUR INVESTMENTS?
5. WHAT IS DOLLAR-COST AVERAGING AND WHAT CAN IT DO?

(THE ANSWERS CAN BE EASILY FOUND IN THIS SECTION)

## 3.   Taxes and Compounding

Governments collect taxes to pay for services such as providing a police force, constructing roads and maintaining them, and running a school system. Some taxes not only raise money – they are also intended to encourage or discourage certain kinds of behaviour. Taxes on cigarettes and alcohol raise money *and* make smoking and drinking less attractive.

The government also uses taxes to encourage certain behaviours. They often offer tax reductions for homeowners because they want to encourage home ownership and the financial responsibility that goes with this, as we saw. Tax reductions that are intended to promote certain actions are known as tax incentives. **Because saving and investing is so important, and because savers play a very important role in the economy, the government uses tax incentives to encourage us to save and invest.**

Some tax incentives, particularly those that relate to pension plans, allow us to put aside a portion of our salaries into stocks or bonds each year, without us having to pay income taxes on the amount contributed. These tax incentives then also allow the savings to compound free of tax. With other plans, money is put aside after income tax has been paid, and *then* the compounding takes place free of taxes. These plans are known as Individual Savings Accounts (ISAs) in the UK, and have various other names in other countries.

Let's look at how taxation impacts compounding, and the amount that we are able to save, if both income and the return are taxed at 40%. For any $1,000 of income that we make, $400 would be taken away in taxes, and the amount that would arrive in our bank account would be $600. Let's see what happens if we save these $600 (which were $1,000 of income before tax) and can earn an average return of 7% per year (that is also taxed). The table below shows how the money will accumulate each year with compounding. The new total at the end of each period is equal to the balance at the start of the year plus the interest, less the taxes.

| YEAR | BALANCE AT START OF YEAR | INTEREST RATE | INTEREST DURING YEAR | TAXES (40%) | TAX GAIN | AFTER CONTRIBUTION AT END OF YEAR | NEW TOTAL AT END OF YEAR |
|------|--------------------------|---------------|----------------------|-------------|----------|-----------------------------------|--------------------------|
| 1 | 0 | 7% | 0.00 | 0.00 | 0.00 | 600.00 | 600.00 |
| 2 | 600.00 | 7% | 42.00 | 16.80 | 25.20 | 600.00 | 1,225.20 |
| 3 | 1,225.20 | 7% | 85.76 | 34.31 | 51.46 | 600.00 | 1,876.66 |
| 4 | 1,876.66 | 7% | 131.37 | 52.55 | 78.82 | 600.00 | 2,555.48 |
| 5 | 2,555.48 | 7% | 178.88 | 71.55 | 107.33 | 600.00 | 3,262.81 |
| 6 | 3,262.81 | 7% | 228.40 | 91.36 | 137.04 | 600.00 | 3,999.85 |
| 7 | 3,999.85 | 7% | 279.99 | 112.00 | 167.99 | 600.00 | 4,767.84 |
| 8 | 4,767.84 | 7% | 333.75 | 133.50 | 200.25 | 600.00 | 5,568.09 |
| 9 | 5,568.09 | 7% | 389.77 | 155.91 | 233.86 | 600.00 | 6,401.95 |
| 10 | 6,401.95 | 7% | 448.14 | 179.25 | 268.88 | 600.00 | **$7,270.83** |

Over the ten years, compounding allows the contributions of $6,000 ($600 x 10) to grow to almost $7,300.

Let's see what happens if we if we can use a tax incentive such as a pension or retirement plan to avoid paying the tax on the $1,000 and on the return. The table below shows how the money compounds over the ten years without taxes.

| YEAR | BALANCE AT START OF YEAR | INTEREST RATE | INTEREST DURING YEAR | CONTRIBUTION AT END OF YEAR | NEW TOTAL AT END OF YEAR |
|------|--------------------------|---------------|----------------------|-----------------------------|--------------------------|
| 1 | 0 | 7% | 0.00 | 1,000.00 | 1,000.00 |
| 2 | 1,000.00 | 7% | 70.00 | 1,000.00 | 2,070.00 |
| 3 | 2,070.00 | 7% | 144.90 | 1,000.00 | 3,214.90 |
| 4 | 3,214.90 | 7% | 225.04 | 1,000.00 | 4,439.94 |
| 5 | 4,439.94 | 7% | 310.80 | 1,000.00 | 5,750.74 |
| 6 | 5,750.74 | 7% | 402.55 | 1,000.00 | 7,153.29 |
| 7 | 7,153.29 | 7% | 500.73 | 1,000.00 | 8,654.02 |
| 8 | 8,654.02 | 7% | 605.78 | 1,000.00 | 10,259.80 |
| 9 | 10,259.80 | 7% | 718.19 | 1,000.00 | 11,977.99 |
| 10 | 11,977.99 | 7% | 838.46 | 1,000.00 | **$13,816.45** |

By contributing $1,000 of our salary every year for ten years, we end up with $13,816.45. In other words, by saving $1,000 of our salary before taxes, we are able to save $13,816.45 as opposed to the $7,270.83 that we were able to save when taxes took away 40% of the income and 40% of the return. The amount that we were able to save is much greater – in fact, in this case 90% greater – almost twice as much! There is usually very little risk of not getting money back when we invest in a pension plan of this type, which is known as a *defined contribution plan*. The amount that we get when we retire is based on what we put in and the returns that we get.

A defined contribution plan does not guarantee any level of benefits at retirement – the benefits depend on our contributions and the return. Plans that guarantee the benefits at retirement are known as *defined benefit plans* and are becoming much less common because they are a large risk for the plan provider (such as the employer) who has to guarantee the benefits. Almost all pension plans that we can get today through our companies and through banks and insurance companies if we are self-employed, are defined contribution plans - what we put in, and our return determine what we get. As we can see, saving money through a pension plan that allows us to save tax on our contributions and on the return, is a very powerful way of increasing the amount of money that we end up with.

For some savings plans like ISAs in the UK, the money that we put in will have been taxed, but it compounds tax free once inside the plan. A $1,000 of salary would again correspond to a contribution of $600, but then the yearly interest would not be taxed. This would look like this:

| YEAR | BALANCE AT START OF YEAR | INTEREST RATE | INTEREST DURING YEAR | CONTRIBUTION AT END OF YEAR | NEW TOTAL AT END OF YEAR |
|---|---|---|---|---|---|
| 1 | 0 | 7% | 0.00 | 600.00 | 600.00 |
| 2 | 600.00 | 7% | 42.00 | 600.00 | 1,242.00 |
| 3 | 1,242.00 | 7% | 86.94 | 600.00 | 1,928.94 |
| 4 | 1,928.94 | 7% | 135.03 | 600.00 | 2,663.97 |
| 5 | 2,663.97 | 7% | 186.48 | 600.00 | 3,450.44 |
| 6 | 3,450.44 | 7% | 241.53 | 600.00 | 4,291.97 |
| 7 | 4,291.97 | 7% | 300.44 | 600.00 | 5,192.41 |
| 8 | 5,192.41 | 7% | 363.47 | 600.00 | 6,155.88 |
| 9 | 6,155.88 | 7% | 430.91 | 600.00 | 7,186.79 |
| 10 | 7,186.79 | 7% | 503.08 | 600.00 | $8,289.87 |

This is less than the amount that we were able to save in the ideal case when the $1,000 *and* the return were not taxed, but it is still almost $1,000 more than we would have saved when both were taxed and no tax incentives were applied. After a longer period of time this difference would be even more important. After twenty years, the tax-free compounding ISA plan would grow to $24,597.30, whereas when the returns are taxed, the amount saved only grows to $18,242.21. As the money compounds for a longer period of time, the fact that the return is not taxed is of greater and greater benefit, as the returns grow and grow with compounding.

Saving the tax on the amount contributed *and* tax on the return is better than just being able to save the tax on the return, but there are often limitations on the amount that can be contributed to the pension type plans that allow both taxes to be saved. Also, because these plans provide a tax incentive to save for retirement, they often have penalties if one needed to withdraw the money before retirement, and we would also usually have to pay tax on money withdrawn before retirement. If the amount withdrawn is taxed, the plan might still save taxes, in that when we paid the money in, we were probably working and paying a high tax rate, and when we are taking it out we might not be working, and our tax rate might be lower. Furthermore, the fact that the money was able to compound tax-free inside the plan is also beneficial.

The most common pension plans allow tax-free contribution and tax-free withdrawal at a certain age. If a saving plan works with money that has already been taxed like ISAs do in the UK, then the money is usually not taxed again at withdrawal (it is not in the case of ISAs). A plan that saves tax just on the return is still a good complement to the pension-type plan that saves tax on both.

With the help of a spreadsheet it is very easy to simulate what the plans would mean for saving over a longer period of time. Effectively any tax saving will ultimately put more money directly into our pockets in a government sponsored and perfectly legal manner. This can have a huge impact on the ultimate amount saved. Tax laws vary between regions, and also change with time depending on what the government is trying to achieve, but the principle is always there – because the government is trying to encourage saving and investing, the incentives described above are usually available. It is worth investigating this by going to the government tax website regarding pensions and savings plans, checking the internet, or by speaking to a reputable financial professional.

**Compounding is very powerful no matter what, and needs to be a foremost consideration when we are thinking about saving and accumulating wealth. Compounding with tax savings can improve the amounts saved even more.**

KEY QUESTIONS THAT WE CAN ANSWER AFTER READING THIS SECTION
(CHECK THAT YOU CAN):

1. WHAT IS A TAX INCENTIVE?
2. WHY DO GOVERNMENTS PROVIDE TAX INCENTIVES FOR SAVING AND INVESTING?
3. WHAT FORMS CAN THESE TAX INCENTIVES TAKE?
4. WHY IS USING THESE TAX INCENTIVES IMPORTANT?

(THE ANSWERS CAN BE EASILY FOUND IN THIS SECTION)

## 4.    DIVERSIFICATION

**Diversification means not putting all of our eggs into one basket.**
Research has shown that when we invest in multiple things that do not move
perfectly together, that the risk/reward relationship can be improved. This
is relevant when we buy more than one stock, multiple bonds, a mixture of
stocks and bonds or a mixture of stocks, bonds and commodities. The less
the assets move together, the better the diversification effect.

The returns of the S&P 500 over any one-year period jump around a lot
as we saw earlier. We can quantify how much the returns jump around by
looking at something called the standard deviation. This is a measure of how
much the yearly returns are dispersed around the average return, and it is
therefore a measure of the risk of the investment. A high standard deviation
for the return of an asset means that the returns can vary significantly from
the average in any given year – in other words, that the risk is higher because
the returns are more volatile. A low standard deviation means that, since the
returns do not deviate that much from the mean, that the return is more
predictable – the risk is lower. For the S&P 500 between 1939 and 2004,
the average return including dividends was about 12.5%, and the standard
deviation of the returns was about 16.8%. The standard deviation of 16.8%
is a very high number, and confirms as we already saw that the annual returns
move around quite a bit.

**Risk-free government bonds have historically offered a lower return, but
the return has also been less volatile.** Neither investment has necessarily
been 'better' – one has had a higher risk and higher return, the other one a
lower risk and lower return – there is a trade-off. Depending on things like
our time horizon, both should play a role.

**We can see the beneficial role that diversification plays by looking at the
returns and the standard deviations of assets as we mix them together.**
For example, we could mix an investment in risk-free government bonds
with the stocks of the S&P 500; alternatively we could mix an investment
in commodities with an investment in the S&P 500. We could also add
emerging market stocks to an investment in the S&P 500. We would expect
that as the portfolio became riskier, that the return and the risk would go
up together. What has happened in reality, over many periods of time, is
that as we added more of the risky assets, the return went up, but the risk, as
measured by the standard deviation, *decreased*.

For example if we take a look at the historical risk and return for the US government bond market and the S&P 500, as we add more and more and more of the riskier equity asset, the result would over many periods look like the one below. The lowest point on the graph represents an investment of 100% government bonds, and as we move up the curve, each point contains more of the S&P 500 and less of the bonds until we reach a point where the portfolio consists entirely of the riskier S&P 500 assets.

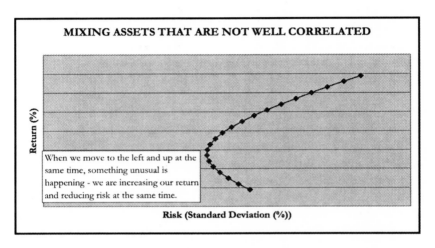

**MIXING ASSETS THAT ARE NOT WELL CORRELATED**

Return (%)

When we move to the left and up at the same time, something unusual is happening - we are increasing our return and reducing risk at the same time.

**Risk (Standard Deviation (%))**

As we can see, as we added more of the riskier asset, and as we move up the curve, on the top section of the curve, the return increases and so does the risk – this is not unexpected. **What is more interesting is that at the bottom of the curve, as we begin to add the riskier asset, the return rises (as we move up the curve) while at the same time risk falls (as the curve moves towards the left).** By adding the stocks to a bond portfolio, we generated more return with less risk! Beautiful! And this is the effect of diversification in action.

**The more the two assets that are combined move in opposite directions, over say one-year periods, the more pronounced this effect is over the longer term. In other words, the more *negatively correlated* the assets are, the more powerful the diversification effect.**

For the US stock and bond markets, adding stock to a bond portfolio has over many periods decreased risk and increased return. Adding bonds to a stock portfolio decreased risk more than it decreased returns.

Bonds with a shorter maturity seem to have a greater impact than long-term bonds in decreasing risk when added to stocks, probably because both long-term bonds and equities have their cash flows further in the future – short-term bonds do not, and therefore have offered better diversification properties. International country indices have also reduced risk while improving the return over certain time periods. If the number of assets that are not well correlated is higher, historically the effect has been observed to be stronger.

If an asset has a higher return *and* a lower risk, then we should clearly buy that one, although this is unlikely to be the case and we are unlikely to be able to predict this if it is the case temporarily. The diversification effect relates more a 'normal' environment where risk is higher when the expected return is higher. In an efficient market, this is the case.

**Mixing higher return, higher risk assets with lower return, lower risk assets has a lot of benefits if the two assets are not well correlated - this is a mathematical fact. To benefit from the diversification effect of the earlier chart,** we have to ask ourselves the following:

- **Do we expect the each asset to produce a return by itself?** If not, there is no point in having the asset in the first place;
- **Are the assets likely to be very correlated or poorly correlated (which is what we want)?** How correlated the assets are depends on two main factors:
  - **Are the investments likely to be affected by the same trends;** for example, the stocks of two companies in a same sector such as the oil sector, are likely to be affected by the same trends. Also, for example, if the real estate market in New York is largely driven by how well the stock market does, then these two assets are likely to be more correlated than one might expect at first thought;
  - **Do the same investors own the assets?** Assets that might fundamentally have nothing to do with each other might have a high correlation because the same buyers determine their prices. For example, if a majority of US investors have turned their attention to the Japanese equity market, then the Japanese equity market would begin to perform more like the US equity market – more so than the fundamentals of the Japanese market would otherwise suggest. If a lot of homeowners in Japan are buying houses in California, then

the correlation of the two real estate markets would also be expected to increase.

**Over time, the correlations between assets change, and assets that have shown a certain correlation in the past, might have a different one in the future. That is why the principle of diversification is more important than the specific historical observations.** In order to benefit from diversification, we always need to think about the correlation of our assets – **if the assets move closely together, even if they are not exactly the same thing – then we have too many eggs in one basket and are not diversified.** If we are exposed to assets that are not that well correlated, and the risk/return relationship is normal, then the diversification effect will work – we will be able to increase return at the same time as decreasing risk, or decrease risk more than we are decreasing return, as in the chart at the beginning of the section - it is just the way that the math works.

The correlation of asset classes can clearly increase over time, thereby decreasing the diversification benefit. For example, the macroeconomic policies of European countries are becoming more similar - in terms of taxation, interest rate policy and so on. The benefits of diversification that might have been obtained many years ago by mixing investments from France and Germany, for example, are decreasing as the performance of the economies and of the two financial markets becomes more similar, and as the correlation between the assets of the two countries increases. Many large French companies probably also do as much business in Germany today as they do in France and vice versa – where the company is based is becoming a less significant factor. As companies and markets become more integrated, the diversification benefit declines, and we might have to look at more distant geographic regions to find the same diversification benefits.

**Another thing that has been observed is that during severe market corrections, diversification works less well than theory would suggest – in other words, it works less well when we need it most.** When markets are crashing, it has been observed that correlations between asset classes rise as investors pull money out of all investments at once. Asset classes that otherwise have very little to do with each other, and usually show great diversification properties, move down together more when they are all being sold at the same time.

All of this means that in order to diversify well, we should err on the side of caution by diversifying more, and by using assets that have less to do with each other than history might suggest. The performance of investments that are less correlated will be driven by different fundamental factors, and the same investors will not own them.

The exercise of selecting different assets to invest in is known as asset allocation. Because to a large extent, individual stock selection, sector selection, and active management in general, are so difficult, and as many researchers argue, a waste of time, asset allocation is probably the most important decision that we can make when it comes to investing. Ideally, the best assets are the ones with a higher return and a lower risk. Given that there is usually 'no free lunch', unfortunately a higher return usually comes with higher risk and diversification is very important if we do not want to run the risk of losing everything.

Diversification is best achieved with a significant number (five or more) of solid long-term asset classes bearing in mind the benefits of index funds, mutually beneficial transactions, compounding, and all the other concepts with which we are now familiar. Clearly, diversification does not make a case for investing in obscure investments where we have no fundamental conviction as to why the investments should go up based on our informed assessment. We can ensure that we are diversified, by investing in equities and bonds from different regions in large part via index funds as discussed earlier (and using dollar cost averaging), real estate and private equity, hedge funds and commodities if we can get access to them and once we have reached a certain level of savings. Even art or other collectibles can play a role in small amounts as we discussed before.

Equities and bonds are very often two core elements of a saving and investing program; determining the exact percentages that we should have equities and bonds, as well as in the other asset classes is more of an art than a science. The first consideration needs to be the risk that we are willing to tolerate, and tied to that, the time horizon for our investments. The earlier charts regarding, the volatility of investments and the S&P 500 are very important to bear in mind. The longer the time horizon, the more we can think about investing in equities. As we saw, as we increased our investment horizon, the returns of the S&P 500 historically averaged out to an increasingly consistent return. In fact, the return for any thirty-year period since the 1930s has been very close to 10% or higher per year – an excellent return. Although these trends have persisted for a very long period of time, the future can be different than the past, although the mutually beneficial relationship that providers and users of capital can have in the stock market, should contribute strongly to this not changing. We can however still not put all of our money into equities even if we have a very long investment horizon - it is just not prudent. Our personal circumstances might change, and we might need more money sooner than we anticipated. If all of our money is in long-term assets that happen to be doing poorly at that very moment, then we have a problem. Furthermore, through diversification we can increase the risk/reward relationship as we saw, and we should definitely make use of this.

As we implement any saving and investing plan, no matter what asset allocation we target, the things that we can be sure about – compounding, dollar cost averaging, tax savings, the benefits of index funds in mature markets, and the benefits of diversification should be in the forefront of our minds at all times.

KEY QUESTIONS THAT WE CAN ANSWER AFTER READING THIS SECTION (CHECK THAT YOU CAN):

1.   WHAT IS DIVERSIFICATION?
2.   HOW CAN WE MEASURE RISK?
3.   WHAT DOES DIVERSIFICATION ALLOW US TO DO?
4.   WHAT ARE THE MAIN CONSIDERATIONS WHEN WE ARE LOOKING TO DIVERSIFY?
5.   WHAT CAN AFFECT THE CORRELATIONS BETWEEN ASSETS?
6.   HOW SHOULD WE THINK ABOUT IMPLEMENTING OUR ASSET ALLOCATION?

(THE ANSWERS CAN BE EASILY FOUND IN THIS SECTION)

## 5. TRANSACTION COSTS

**When we make investments, sell investments or even hold investments over time, there are typically costs involved. These costs, like taxes, come directly out of the return that flows into our pockets. Some costs are unavoidable and justified - some are not. As we saw earlier, improving our return a little bit per year can make a big difference over a longer period of time, so avoiding unnecessary charges can be very important.**

**First of all, it is clearly always in our best interest to reduce transaction costs wherever possible, all other things being equal.** A lot of this can be done by shopping around and making sure that we understand the costs involved in a product. For example, some mortgages have lower rates than others, but they might come with set-up fees or early repayment penalties etcetera. Some credit cards come with annual fees even if we pay the balance off each month; others don't and even give us cash back or other benefits when we spend. Similarly, some mutual funds have high fees when we purchase them, and for each year that we hold them – others like most index funds do not have the upfront fees, and have lower annual fees. Spending a small amount of time thinking about transaction costs before each investment decision can save a lot of money, especially if the fees are recurring. Recurring fees reduce the rate at which we compound our money each year, and accordingly they can affect the outcome over many years dramatically.

Furthermore, as we saw when we discussed mental accounting, saving two hundred dollars on a major investment is as good as buying something that usually costs $300 for $100. In other words, just because we might be dealing with larger numbers, does not mean we should not worry about saving what might seem like a relatively small amount of money.

**When it comes to the actual transaction costs on savings products, the first key is to understand what the fees are for.** Mutual funds or unit trusts usually have an annual management fee, and sometimes even upfront fees or back-end fees. Upfront fees are percentages that we have to pay for entering the fund, and back-end fees are fees for exiting the fund. For developed markets, where there is generally no benefit in paying for active management, we can reduce the management fees by using index funds. The upfront and back-end fees also have to be looked at; these typically have no justification, and most index funds also completely avoid these charges. Saving the two charges and reducing the management fee will have a significant effect on the overall performance of the investment over the long term.

Buying individual stocks or bonds, requires detailed thought, and some analysis of each investment. For many of us, buying index funds is a better alternative. If we do decide to buy individual stocks or bonds, then transaction costs can often be greatly reduced by shopping around and paying only for the things that we value like good executions, as opposed to paying for a lot of research that in many cases does not add value.

In more distant and exotic markets such as some emerging markets, there might be market access charges to buy investments in those markets. These might be perfectly justifiable and unavoidable. The key is to ensure that they are unavoidable, and if they are, and we really want to invest in that region, then so be it. It could very well also be a good idea to pay for active management in these markets because they might still be relatively inefficient, and a portfolio manager through his work might be able to add quite a bit of value.

**There is nothing wrong with paying for a value-added service, and in fact that is the basis for our entire economic system.** Paying someone to do something better than we would be able to do it, or at a lower cost, makes a lot of sense. Paying for active management of emerging market securities or private equity investments, or for a hedge fund that is active in an area that we would otherwise not be active in, might for example make very good sense. Paying for an actively managed mutual fund in a developed market, that is likely to underperform the index, is probably not justifiable when low cost index funds are available from reputable product providers.

<u>KEY QUESTIONS THAT WE CAN ANSWER AFTER READING THIS SECTION</u>
<u>(CHECK THAT YOU CAN)</u>:

1. WHY ARE TRANSACTION COSTS IMPORTANT?
2. WHAT ARE THE MOST COMMON AVOIDABLE TRANSACTION COSTS?
3. SHOULD WE SPEND A FEW MINUTES UNDERSTANDING THE TRANSACTION COSTS OF INVESTMENTS?
4. WHAT KINDS OF TRANSACTION COSTS ARE JUSTIFIABLE?

(THE ANSWERS CAN BE EASILY FOUND IN THIS SECTION)

# Chapter VI

# GETTING STARTED

**So far we have covered a very comprehensive set of topics:**

COMPOUNDING
DEBT, EQUITY AND FINANCIAL MARKETS
INVESTMENTS
- Debt and Bonds (Fixed Income Investments)
- Equity and Stocks
- Mutual Funds or Unit Trusts
- Hedge Funds
- Real Estate
- Commodities
- Other Investments
THE ECONOMY
SAVING AND INVESTING IN PRACTICE
- The Impact of Time
- Timing Investments and Dollar Cost Averaging
- Taxes and Compounding
- Diversification
- Transaction Costs

**By understanding and applying these concepts, we will be able to travel far on the road to making better investment decisions and towards financial freedom.** Ultimately, we will have to take decisions ourselves about what we are going to do with this knowledge, and take actions based on our means, our goals and our preferences. For each one of us this will probably mean slightly different things; each one of us has also probably been doing some things well and others not so well. **It is worth going through the areas covered, thinking about them, and noting down some of the actions that we need to take for ourselves.**

**For most of us, we can safely do a lot of what is required to be effective savers ourselves. We can eliminate high interest rate debt, start saving through regular automatic contributions, use index funds, make use of tax savings, diversify our investments and so on.** Getting on the road to financial freedom will take a few decisions and a very manageable amount of set-up time. **All we have to do is be proactive and take some action!**

**Choosing to start saving in a proper manner today will have huge impact on our lives in twenty years' time.** Just as starting a healthier lifestyle today will have huge impact on our lives in twenty years as well. We cannot get to all of our goals overnight, but we can certainly set the foundation for attaining them, take small steps on a regular basis, and see the a huge improvement over time.

**Keeping a long-term focus is crucial. The long-term is where we are going to end up by definition.** Our worst decisions will be made by acting without thinking first, or by letting a moment of fear or greed determine what we do. Fear and greed definitely lead to some of the worst investment decisions. So much so that scams and get-rich-quick schemes that are doomed to fail play on exactly these two emotions. The fear of missing something, an empty promise of riches with no effort – if it were that easy, there would be no point in making any effort, and the people touting these schemes would probably be on a beach somewhere, as opposed to wasting their time trying to sell something to us. **On the other hand, fundamentally valid investment concepts that we have learned about will withstand the test of time - so much so that they are to a large extent the very basis of how our society interacts.**

Finally, as we set off on our journey of financial development, we should bear in mind a few more things:

- We will need a *positive outlook* and *courage* to stick to our beliefs and to our savings plan, and in some cases, not to go along with the crowd blindly. Investments that everyone else is chasing madly are usually destined to fail;
- We need to be *flexible* and *accept some uncertainty* since in a lot of investing there is no certainty - especially in the short-term, and especially with volatile investments. There can inevitably be times when we lose money. The key is to lose money less often than we make it, to learn from the things that went wrong, not to bet everything in one go, and most importantly to use those aspects of the financial world that we can be sure about - compounding, tax savings, diversification, the impact of time and dollar cost averaging;
- *We need to be prepared to learn from others.* There is no monopoly on good ideas, and we can never have enough idols and role models to inspire us. Surrounding ourselves with people that have positive beliefs and desires can really help push us. Furthermore, very few things have not been done before, and someone else's insights or opinion can be incredibly valuable.

**Ultimately, although we are focused on our finances, giving back to others can be one of the greatest ways to raise the standard for ourselves and to earn a return. Making a contribution and adding value are two elements that are crucial to anyone's real success.** We can teach others by giving time, or we can give money to important causes. Both can make a difference and be very rewarding emotionally as well.

**One thing that we sometimes need to be reminded of is that if we want to change our circumstances, changing ourselves is a good place to start.** Doing the same things that we always do will probably lead to the same results. In order to change the result, or accomplish any new goal, we need to do things better and focus on improving how we do things, and therefore improve how we effectively are. By learning and applying the rules of finance as they have been detailed in this book, we have already taken a huge step forward with respect to improving our financial outcome. To stay ahead, we need to implement this knowledge and continue to learn and improve. **The best way of doing this is by thinking about saving and investing continuously, applying our financial skills to take informed actions, and by building on or financial knowledge as we go forward as well.**

Outside investment advisors can also be a source of opinions and potentially good ideas and products. The key is for us to be able to consider their inputs intelligently and as informed investors. Investment advisers at reputable institutions generally mean well and have knowledge – **but so do we if we are familiar with all of the topics discussed in this book. Additionally, we will probably always care more about our money than most other people will. Most people care about their own money more than they do about anyone else's no matter what the circumstances.** Furthermore, the reality is that the compensation of professional advisers usually does not depend on whether we are compounding and saving effectively over the long-term, but rather on the products that they sell to us in the short-term.

**As we approach the end of this book, it might be worth saying that we all know that many of us enjoy shopping.** What is important is that we are shopping with our excess cash and saving and investing first - not the other way around. We should have an automated plan in place that maximises the benefits of all of the concepts that we have learned about; beyond that, we can even think of making investments in stocks, bonds, funds, real estate, commodities and other investments as *shopping*. For a lot of people shopping for investments has become one of their most rewarding hobbies – emotionally and financially. Buying a fund through dollar cost averaging for our savings that we can watch grow is more fun than watching our debt grow after purchasing something that quickly becomes worthless. Often when we buy clothing or jewellery, we look forward to purchasing the item for weeks, are extremely pleased when we purchase it, and after a few days or weeks do not even care about it any more. **This empty feeling is one that we will not end up with when we buy investments that go up over the long term. These purchases can be a real source of satisfaction and pride for a very long time. Not to mention that they are necessary – saving money and managing our finances is important stuff - one of the most important things in our lives!**

**Ultimately, accumulating money over the long-term, will allow us to buy many things. But not only that, along the way we get to understand and discuss concepts that affect a large part of the world around us, apply interesting methods and show some discipline. The journey should be fun and rewarding in and of itself – the goal of course being financial freedom. Although it rarely appears that way ahead of time, often the greatest source of satisfaction is not the final result itself, but the journey towards it, although the final result will undeniably arrive as well.**

# Some Key Saving and Investing Terms

**ANNUAL REPORT**
A company's annual summary of their operations, which typically includes an income statement, balance sheet and a cash flow statement. The report comes with footnotes detailing how things were accounted for. An independent auditor usually checks it.

**ASSET**
Something of value that an individual, a company or other institution owns. Assets can be thought of as things that generate economic value. For a company, assets are things like buildings and equipment that the company owns. On a balance sheet, assets are usually shown on the left side, and they match the sources of funding on the right side.

**BALANCE SHEET**
A summary of a company's assets (usually on the left side) and the sources of funding – equity and debt (on the right side) at a point in time for example, the end of the year. The two sides balance and hence the name.

**BOND**
A piece or slice of debt.

**BONDHOLDER**
The owner of a bond.

**CASH FLOW STATEMENT**
A financial statement that records a company's actual cash flows – the cash that is coming into and going out of the company. The cash flow statement is usually split into three sections that separate where the cash flows occur – in operations, investing and financing.

**CENTRAL BANK**
The bank that acts on behalf of the overall country. Central banks have numerous functions, the main one often being the control of inflation, which is often done through adjustments to interest rates. The central bank also usually controls the money supply of an economy.

**COMPOUNDING**
Repeatedly earning a return on a sum of money. As each return is added, the sum grows and each subsequent return is larger causing the sum of money to grow faster and faster.

**COUPON**
A regular usually fixed pre-determined payment associated with a bond that the bondholder receives for making the money available. It helps determine the interest or the return or yield on the bond.

**DEBT**
An amount of money that is borrowed by one party and lent by the other.

**DIVIDEND**
A portion of the net income of a company that is paid out to the shareholders usually in the form of cash.

**DOLLAR COST AVERAGING**
Investing the same amount of money periodically on a regular basis. It is a way of lowering the average purchase price since more units are bought when prices are lower and less when prices are higher.

**EBITDA**
Earnings before Interest Taxes Depreciation and Amortisation. EBITDA is a measure of the operating earnings of a company.

### ENTERPRISE VALUE
The market value of a company's equity plus the net debt of the company (debt minus cash).

### EQUITY
The ownership interest that investors have. It is the asset value minus any debt.

### HEDGE FUND
An absolute return fund that is managed by a hedge fund manager to generate returns for the investors that have contributed money to the fund. Hedge funds are more flexible in what they can do versus other funds; they usually short-sell investments and also frequently employ leverage to generate returns.

### INCOME STATEMENT
A summary of a company's revenues, costs and ultimately net income or profits over a certain period of time, typically one year.

### INDEX FUND
A mutual fund that mirrors an index. Investment decisions are made automatically to maintain the weights of the investments as closely as possible to the weights within the index. An index fund is considered to be passively managed.

### INFLATION
The rise in the price of goods and services over a certain period like one year.

### LEVERAGE
The use of debt or other means to increase the amount of financial impact that an investor has. Leverage using debt magnifies returns both on the upside as well as the downside.

### MONEY MARKET
A financial market for short-term debt of one-year maturity or less.

### MUTUAL FUND
A pool of money that is invested by a professional fund manager to generate returns on behalf the investors that have contributed money to the fund.

## NET INCOME

The profits of a company that are left over once all expenses have been subtracted from the sales or revenues of a company over a certain period of time, for example one year. The net income can be retained by the company (retained earnings) in which case the book value of the equity rises by the amount of the retained earnings, or paid out to shareholders as a dividend, usually in the form of cash.

## REAL RETURN

The return to an investor after adjusting for the effects of inflation.

## RETURN

The gain or loss of an investment over a certain period of time, like for example a year. The return is usually expressed as a percentage of the original investment.

## SHARE

A slice of the equity of a company.

## SHORT-SALE

The sale of a security without actually owning it in order to benefit from a decline in the price of the investment. This is done by borrowing the investment from the actual owner and selling it in the market. Money before expenses will be made if the investment can be bought back at a lower price later. Once the investment has been bought back it is returned to the original owner.

## STOCK

A slice of the equity of a company.

## SHAREHOLDER

The owner of a share.

## YIELD

For a bond, the annual total rate of expected return expressed as a percentage. For a stock, the dividend yield is that part of the expected return that comes from the dividends, expressed as a percentage of the stock price.

# Acknowledgements

I would like to thank all of the people that helped me in getting this book to its current form by proof-reading it, commenting on it and perhaps most importantly by offering support and encouragement.

These people include my partner Monique Johnson, my parents Ingo and Christiane Fischer, and my sisters Alex and Julia Fischer, as well as Vincent Barnouin, Christophe Beauvilain, Marsha Bousquet, Nick Bowden, Anna Holland, Dennis Low, Chris Keogh, Thomas Kirkwood, Peter Mallinson, Roger Metta, Daniel Novelli and Ron Westdorp. I would also like to thank Mount Capital in this regard.

I would also like to thank my publishers, Authorhouse, for enabling me to communicate these thoughts and concepts in this manner.

Thank you all very much – I really appreciated it at the time of writing and I appreciate it even more today; I hope that the end product meets and perhaps even exceeds your expectations.

Michael Fischer

# About The Author

**The author is an experienced investment professional who has been providing investment advice and helping some of the largest private banks, mutual fund companies and hedge funds in the world make investment choices for the last ten years.** Specifically, he:

- Worked for nine years at Goldman Sachs and one year at Credit Suisse First Boston in Sales and Trading;
- Was consistently ranked as the top adviser by his clients and peers;
- Bought and sold billions of dollars of investment products on behalf of his clients and himself;
- Is accredited as a Chartered Financial Analyst and has taught this material to candidates taking the tests.

The author also holds an MBA from INSEAD, and an Honors Bachelor of Science degree from the University of Toronto. He is a member of the UK Society of Investment Professionals, and has been on the Advisory Council of the CFA/INSEAD Global Investor's Workshop. He has been a speaker on this subject at numerous venues and conferences. He holds the Series 3, 7, and

63 accreditations from the National Association of Securities Dealers in the United States and is a Registered Representative with the Securities and Futures Authority in the United Kingdom.

Michael left Goldman Sachs in February 2005 to focus on investment management, but before starting out formally, he wanted to address a problem - every week in almost every country you can read in the newspaper about issues such as:

- Misselling of products;
- Savers not saving enough because they do not feel confident with the products;
- Government initiatives to help people save not being taken up, even though they are very beneficial, because people do not have enough confidence to take action;
- Investors making bad choices because they were never taught the basics;
- Kids not having a clue about finance although they are taught so many other things.

Everyone needs to know about this subject. In today's society, finance and the interaction between the different financial players including savers, is in many ways the basis of how much of our society interacts and functions. Without understanding this subject, much of what goes on in the world just passes us by. **Perhaps most importantly, without knowledge of this subject, private individuals will not have the necessary knowledge to achieve their saving and investing dreams.**

**If you don't learn about it and get involved you are selling yourself short. You need to know about this stuff no matter what you do. It is too important to ignore!**

**This is not about greed, short-cuts, opinions or speculation – this is about being an informed participant in the financial system, and about the rewards for participating in order to provide a better life for yourself and others.**

For more information see www.SavingandInvesting.com

Printed in the United Kingdom
by Lightning Source UK Ltd.
134228UK00002B/148/A